USMC TANK MARKINGS IN THE PACIFIC

CASEMATE | ILLUSTRATED | SPECIAL

CASEMATE | ILLUSTRATED | SPECIAL

USMC TANK MARKINGS IN THE PACIFIC

ROMAIN CANSIÈRE

Dedication

This book is dedicated to my friend and mentor, Oscar E. "Ed" Gilbert Jr. (1946–2019)

CISS0022

Published in 2025 by
CASEMATE PUBLISHERS
1950 Lawrence Road, Havertown, PA 19083, USA
and
47 Church Street, Barnsley, S70 2AS, UK

This book is published in cooperation with, and under license from, Sophia Histoire & Collections. Originally published in French as *Les Marquages des Chars du Marine Corps dans la Pacifique* by Romain Cansière

Print Edition: ISBN 978-1-63624-586-7
Digital Edition: ISBN 978-1-63624-587-4

Translated from the French by Alan McKay
Design by Myriam Bell Design, UK
Artwork by Eric Schwartz
Maps by Histoire & Collections
Printed and bound in the Czech Republic by FINIDR s.r.o.

CASEMATE PUBLISHERS (US)
Telephone (610) 853-9131
Fax (610) 853-9146
Email: casemate@casematepublishers.com
www.casematepublishers.com

CASEMATE PUBLISHERS (UK)
Telephone (0)1226 734350
Email: casemate@casemateuk.com
www.casemateuk.com

Author's note: This book contains many official photographs. Some, in order to present the details of the motifs, have been deliberately enlarged. Other shots come from private collections, taken with commercial cameras by inexperienced photographers and developed in conditions that were not always the best for developing films—humidity and temperature. Finally, certain photos come from unrestored period color films. All these photos have been chosen and kept because they are relevant, showing the colors and the markings of the tanks. As a result, in certain cases, these elements are responsible for the reduced quality of the pictures as used in the book. The author accepts full responsibility for this as well as for any mistakes that have slipped into these pages.

Please note that illustrations of tanks are not to scale.

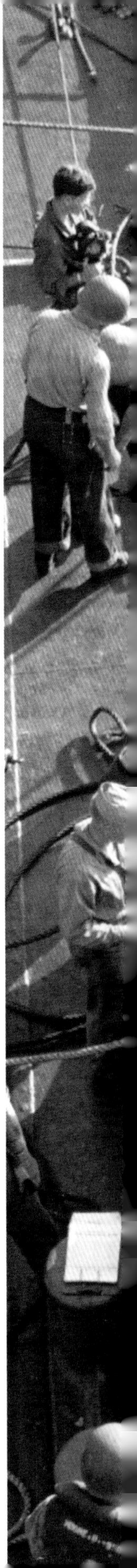

Contents

Introduction

The markings on the U.S. Marine Corps (USMC) tanks during World War II are known for their variety. They are complex and varied and this has led some people to conclude that they had no meaning—that they were even anarchic.

Although official documents on the subject are rare, studying the period photographs and films, and tying them in with the various combat reports and veterans' eye-witness accounts, enable us to reveal the different systems the fighting units used to identify their vehicles.

These markings do indeed vary from one unit to another and from one campaign to another, but they were nonetheless thought out so that they would be practical and easy to interpret—at least for the tankmen.

In most cases, complementing the tactical markings was the tank's name. The crew chose the name; it was subject to the tank commander who had the last word. The practice of humanizing the tank tended to boost crew morale and increase the attention they paid to looking after the materiel. Replacing the tanks more or less regularly was, in fact, a source of discontent for the crews.

This book draws up an inventory, explains the markings used by the USMC's tank fighting units during the Pacific War, from 1942 to 1945, and gives their origin and how they evolved during the conflict.

1 The 1st Tank Battalion

The 1st Tank Battalion was created at New River (North Carolina) on May 1, 1941, two months after the 1st Marine Division to which it was attached. A Company was the redesignation of the USMC's 3rd Tank Company, created in November 1940 when the Marine Corps was timidly starting to develop its own armored arm.

The other companies (B, C, D, and E) were built up gradually until September 1942, as and when the materiel and the personnel became available.

The 1st Marine Division had been transferred to New Zealand in July 1942 in anticipation of being engaged in the South Pacific in the coming months, but Japanese expansion to the south of the Solomon Islands, and the building of an airfield on the Island of Guadalcanal, obliged the Americans to deploy the division hurriedly.

Elements of the 1st Tank Battalion thus reinforced the division's assault troops in the fighting on Guadalcanal, then in New Britain (Cape Gloucester, Arawe, and Talasea), New Guinea (with landings at Aitape and at Humboldt), Peleliu, Ngesebus, and Okinawa. The 1st Tank Battalion was stationed at Tientsin, in China, after the war until 1947, when it was repatriated to Guam, then to the United States on May 1, 1947.

Guadalcanal (August–November 1942)

On Guadalcanal, A and B Companies were respectively equipped with M2A4 and M3 light tanks. C, D, and E Companies (which did not exist yet) did not take part in the fighting on the island. Although a company's standard allocation was some 18 tanks, A Company had 20.[1]

During the Guadalcanal campaign, the markings of the 1st Tank Battalion tanks were inspired by the ones the U.S. Army had used pre-war. These consisted of a series of geometric shapes for designating platoons:

A triangle for HQ Platoon.
A square for 1st Platoon.
A circle for 2nd Platoon.
A diamond for 3rd Platoon.

An M2A4 exercising in the United States. The diamond on the turret indicates a tank belonging to 3rd Platoon. The color stripes were not yet in use and the only way of identifying A Company was by the type of armor. B Company was then equipped with M3 tanks. (NARA via Ken Estes)

1 Some sources indicate that only 18 M2A4 tanks were deployed on Guadalcanal. The two extra tanks in A Company were probably a different model (M3).

Above: An M2A4 from the 1st Tank Battalion during a landing exercise at New River. The square on the turret indicates the 1st Platoon, 4th vehicle, as shown by the number. Also visible on the turret is the registration number T11, an early format in use on USMC tanks. These tanks, when received from the factory, were painted olive drab. They were entirely repainted a matt forest green in conformity with a 1941 Directive. (NARA via Ken Estes)

Above: This photo of Square 5 from A Company shows the typical markings at the beginning of the battle for Guadalcanal. The company stripe on the upper part of the turret only covered the rear. The tank has not yet had the white star painted on the side of its turret. (NARA)

Right: Square 2, an M3 from the 1st Platoon, B Company, 1st Tank Battalion, is lowered into its landing barge on the morning of August 7, 1942. Note that the colored stripe on the front of the turret is absent. The significance of the letter B on the turret remains obscure. This marking was also present on several M2A4s in A Company. (NARA)

Another M2A4 from 1st Platoon, A Company, being loaded aboard an LCM (Landing Craft Mechanized) on August 7, 1942, off Guadalcanal. As can be seen, the yellow stripe does not yet go right round the turret. (USMC HD)

Right: This regularly published photo shows three tanks from the 1st Tank Battalion on Guadalcanal. We can see Square 2 of B Company (second tank in the line) with late markings: the color stripe has been extended along the sides and front of the turret, to make identification easier. The other two vehicles, M2A4s from A Company, also have yellow stripes extending all around the turret. Broad letters have been added on the sides of the turret, probably to replace the triangle, the symbol of HQ Platoon, barely visible on the turret of the first tank. (NARA via Ken Estes)

A number was painted inside each shape indicating the tank's position within the platoon. Thus, number 1 designated the platoon leader or the company commander; number 2 designated the platoon sergeant or the executive officer. The numbers 3, 4, and 5 indicated the three other tanks in the platoon.

The geometric shape and the number were traditionally painted white on the rear and sides of the turret. From time to time, the shape–number combination was painted on the front and rear of the tank's hull. As all the companies used the same marking system, they had to be able to distinguish one from another. Thus, a colored stripe was used to differentiate the companies: yellow for A Company, and red (or rather light red) for B Company. The stripe was painted on the rear of the turret, its size and height varying from one vehicle to another. A (full) square the same color was also painted on the rear of the hull with a T painted white in its center designating "Tanks."[2] Several tanks also had five-point stars painted on each side of the turret.

The USMC registration numbers (unique to each vehicle) were painted white on both sides of the turret or the hull. A Company still had the old 1941 format: a T (for Tanks) followed by a number like T11, T20, T25, etc. Research carried out by historian

[2] The colored square was widely used in A Company. Its use is not attested in B Company.

Left: Maintaining vehicles on Guadalcanal was made difficult by the lack of infrastructure. This rear view of an M2A4 from HQ Platoon of A Company shows the combination of old and new markings applied to the tanks. The (yellow) square with the white T for "Tanks" is still visible next to the imposing HQ painted red on the hull and the turret. The letter A next to the square has probably been added during the campaign and probably designated the company. (USMC HD)

M2 AND M3 LIGHT TANKS FROM THE 1ST TANK BATTALION 1940–1941

M2A4, Circle 2, 1st Platoon, A Company, Guadalcanal, August 1942.

M3, Circle 5, 2nd Platoon, B Company, Guadalcanal, September 1942.

Right: The dense Guadalcanal jungle was unfavorable to tanks. During most of the campaign, they were kept near Henderson Field, half-buried for protection against shrapnel from Japanese bombs. Their role during the campaign was mainly defensive. This image shows Circle 2, an M3 (diesel) from 2nd Platoon, B Company. (NARA)

Below: Square 5 from A Company seen here being hoisted aboard the ship which was to take it to Australia after Guadalcanal. Note the added white stars, the extended yellow stripe around and on top of the turret, as well as the name *The Blizzard* added on the side. (USMC HD)

Kenneth W. Estes (see Bibliography) shows that the use of the prefix T goes back to the end of the 1930s, when the Marine Corps was only equipped with Marmon-Herrington tankettes. Numbers T1 to T10 were attributed to these vehicles. At the end of 1940, when the first 18 M2A4s were received, they were attributed with numbers T11 to T28. In January 1941, the second batch of 18 M2A4s was given the numbers T29 to T46. Both batches were respectively assigned to A Company of the 1st Tank Battalion and A Company of the 2nd Tank Battalion (which did not use them in combat). The use of the T-numbers stopped with T46.

B Company used a more recent arrangement of registration numbers: a set of five numbers starting with 60 and beginning with USMC (USMC 60133, for example). This numbering system appeared in 1941 and replaced the T-numbers. On the sides of the hull was a code consisting of two letters and three numbers. The prefixes MA and MC were used and probably referred to "Marine Corps." Examples like MA102, MA202, and MC301 were respectively visible on the tanks of A, B, and C Companies.

After the battle of the Tenaru (August 21, 1942) tank markings evolved slightly.

The color stripe identifying the companies was extended all around the turret to make the vehicle easier to identify, no matter what angle it was observed from.

In the case of A Company, HQ Platoon tanks had prominent markings added to those already present. The letters HQ were painted in red on the rear of the vehicle (turret and hull) and the letters C and S were painted on the turret sides, also in red. The letter C designates a Company Command tank and the S an executive officer's vehicle (Staff).[3]

Above: This photo shows a hybrid M3, a transition model between the M3 and the M3A1. Despite what has been previously written, this photo was not taken at Guadalcanal but on Samoa some time before the battle. It is a C Company tank. (USMC HD)

3 The term "staff" was occasionally used by the Marine Corps to designate the executive officer.

New Britain and New Guinea (December 1943–April 1944)

In order to successfully encircle the Rabaul bastion, MacArthur asked the 1st Marine Division to support the U.S. Army as it advanced towards the Western Solomon Islands. In exchange, the U.S. Army agreed to reequip the division with new, modern equipment. For the 1st Tank Battalion, this meant obtaining new medium M4A1 and light M5A1 tanks.

The tanks, painted olive drab, were still painted with five-point stars and for some of them, with their registration number in the Army format.

Meanwhile, the USMC reorganized its tank battalions and decided to use a company of medium tanks for two companies of light tanks.

Within the 1st Tank Battalion, this became a reality when A Company was equipped with 18 M4A1 Shermans,[4] and B and C Companies were equipped with 18 M5A1s each.

After the white stars had been covered, A Company numbered its Shermans 1–18 with tanks 1–5 belonging to the 1st Platoon, 6–10 to the 2nd Platoon, 11–15 to the 3rd Platoon. Tanks numbered 16, 17, and 18 belonged to the HQ Platoon. The numbers were painted white on the four corners of the turrets except for the HQ Platoon which did not paint the numbers on its tanks. The tank number was painted on the engine compartment access doors, and was preceded by the company letter (A).

The tactical markings of the other two companies are less well-known. Period photos, specifically those showing the rear of the vehicles, are lacking.

However, it seems that B Company tanks had no markings, whereas the M5A1s in C Company had the vehicle number painted white on the center of the upper part of the glacis and on the hull sides.

During the landing on Aitape in New Guinea, the men in A Company[5] added the USMC symbol (eagle, globe, and anchor) with a stencil on the turret sides, and between the driver and assistant driver's hatches. From time to time, the vehicle was given a name which was painted on the sides or the rear of the hull, on the gun barrel, or on the turret sides.

4 22 M4A1s were supplied to the USMC, but only 18 were deployed. Once again, the company was overequipped since the standard allocation at the time for a medium tank company was 14 vehicles.

5 Only A Company took part in this landing.

An M4A1 from A Company, training in Australia. It still has the U.S. Army's five-point white star on the turret. It is one of the 22 M4A1s taken from the army stocks for the USMC. (NARA)

Above: B Company of the 1st Tank Battalion was the first USMC tank unit to use flamethrowers in combat, at Arawe, New Britain. It was a portable infantry (Model M1A1) flamethrower mounted in place of the hull machine gun. Note the absence of markings on this M5A1, typical of this unit. (NARA)

Below left: An M5A1 from C Company, 1st Tank Battalion, on a trail at Cape Gloucester in December 1943. Note the number of the tank painted white on the upper part of the glacis and the hull flanks. Other inscriptions are visible on the flanks but remain illegible. (USMC HD)

Below right: A Company of the 1st Tank Battalion was the only USMC unit to use the M4A1 model. Note the five-point white star of the U.S. Army has been covered with olive-drab paint. This photo was taken in New Britain and shows a vehicle without a tactical number. This indicates that it is one of the three HQ tanks of A Company. (USMC HD)

Left: The M5A1s of B Company had no markings on the front and sides during the battle of Arawe. The lack of photos showing the rear of the vehicles does not enable us to say whether markings were used or not. (NARA)

Below: Within A Company, the tank number was painted white on the four corners of the turret. The tactical marking made up of the company letter followed by the tank number was also painted on the engine access doors, as this image shows. (USMC HD)

Top: An M5A1 from C Company approaching Cape Gloucester. Note the camouflage on the turret, made up of large patches of earth brown on the factory-painted olive drab. On the rear part of the hull we can see what is left of the former U.S. Army registration number which has been covered with paint by the crew. (USMC HD)

Middle: Marines posing on their M4A1 after the battle for Cape Gloucester. Note the two-tone camouflage (olive drab and black) used on the vehicle. (USMC HD)

Below: This other photograph taken at Cape Gloucester shows the camouflage used by A Company during the campaign. (NARA via Ken Estes)

M4 MEDIUM TANKS FROM THE 1ST TANK BATTALION, 1944

M4A1, A-11, *Bloody Bastard*, 3rd Platoon, A Company, New Guinea, April 1944.

M4A2 (late), B5, 2nd Platoon, B Company, Peleliu, September 1944.

Above: This image of a tank depot, waiting for repatriation to the United States to be scrapped, shows M4A1s from A Company on the left, as well as M5A1s from C Company on the right. The camouflage used by the two units can clearly be seen. Note also the USMC emblem painted yellow on the turret of the M4A1 number 9, added for the landing on Aitape. Other markings have been added after the tanks were stored here. (David Doyle)

Left: An M4A1 from the 1st Platoon of A Company in the dense jungle of New Britain. The tactical markings are clearly visible. (NARA)

Peleliu, Ngesebus (September–October 1944) and Okinawa (April–June 1945)

In the summer of 1944, the Marine Corps reorganized its tank units. From then on, they were entirely equipped with Sherman medium tanks. The 1st Tank Battalion received diesel M4A2s, 15 per company plus an M32B2 recovery vehicle on a Sherman chassis.[6] Another novelty, one Sherman per company was now fitted with a bulldozer blade. The battalion included three tank companies (A, B, and C) with 15 Shermans each, shared out in five platoons, plus the M4A2 of the battalion commanding officer in the Headquarters and Service Company / H&S Co.

After the 1st Tank Battalion received its M4A2s, the markings were harmonized. A letter-number combination was adopted, showing the company letter (A, B, or C) followed by the tank number. The numbering of the tanks was then sequential. With three tanks in a platoon, the tanks were therefore numbered: 1–3 for 1st Platoon; 4–6 for 2nd Platoon; 7–9 for 3rd Platoon; 10–12 for 4th Platoon, and 13–15 for HQ Platoon. The tankdozer was systematically No. 14, the recovery vehicle No. 16, and was placed in the Maintenance Section of HQ Platoon.

6 The Marine Corps made wide use of the diesel version of the Sherman (M4A2) because it was the first model to be rapidly available in large quantities.

An M4A2 from A Company taking a break on Peleliu airfield in September 1944. During the operation, some vehicles had a little pennant at the end of the radio antennae. There were three colors (red, black, and white) which probably indicated the company. (NARA via Morgan Gillard)

Above: At Peleliu, the 1st Tank Battalion was entirely re-equipped with M4A2 Shermans. The markings consisted of a sequence of letters and numbers painted only on the four corners of the turret. The USMC registration number and the radio model equipping the tank were painted on the hull side. On the front part of the hull sides, the battalion symbol—the profile of a bulldog's head—was covered with a thick layer of paint on most vehicles. (USMC HD)

Left: Only a handful of tanks from C Company were able to take part in the fighting on Peleliu due to lack of transport ships. The tank markings were painted white except for the registration number, which was yellow. (NARA via Ed Gilbert)

Above: The battalion insignia is still visible on B5 photographed on Peleliu airfield. On this example, the tactical number has been repositioned after the steel links were welded onto the turret. This improvised armor was there mainly to prevent small arms ammunition from piercing the turret. (USMC HD)

Below: The tankdozer from A Company is seen protecting Marine riflemen on Peleliu. The Marine at the rear of the tank is giving information to the tankmen via the field telephone located inside the grouser's box at the rear of the tank (the black oval shape). This device appeared on Peleliu in the case of A Company. (Corporal John F. Naut, USMCR via Michael J. Livingston)

Above: A rear view of an M4A2 on Peleliu still equipped with the base of the fording kit. As with the field telephone, the fording kit appeared on Peleliu with the 1st Tank Battalion and was a real innovation. (Corporal John F. Naut, USMCR via Michael J. Livingston)

Below: Another photo of an M4A2 from C Company on Peleliu. Note the effectiveness and clarity of the tactical marking on the turret. The tank belongs to the 3rd Platoon. (NARA via Ed Gilbert)

Above: After Peleliu, the 1st Tank Battalion was redirected to the rear base Pavuvu in the Solomon Islands. The crews—here that of B13, nicknamed *Liz*—are busy getting the materiel reconditioned. Unlike other units, the 1st Tank Battalion kept its M4A2s for Okinawa. (NARA)

Left: The steel track links welded onto the glacis and turret proved effective against Japanese small-caliber projectiles during the battle of Peleliu. The use of extra protection continued during the next campaign. (NARA)

The letter–number association was painted white on the four corners of the turret. On the hull sides were painted: the registration number in the USMC format, e.g. "USMC 100450" (yellow); the type of radio equipping the vehicle (SCR 508 or SCR 528) (white); and a series of numbers (4-G-4644 or 4-G-4383) also painted white, but whose meaning remains a mystery.

In B Company, a white five-point star was painted on the commander's hatch for aerial identification. These markings seemed unique to this company. At least one M4A2 in this company also had the battalion's symbol painted on the front of the hull side: a white bulldog's head.[7] This symbol was covered by a heavy layer of green paint on the other vehicles in the battalion.

Most of the tanks in B and C Companies could not be loaded for the battle of Peleliu–Ngesebus because there were not enough transport ships. Only nine M4A2s of B Company and six Shermans from C Company took part in the fighting.

At the end of 1944 when the Marine Corps started converting its tank battalions to the gasoline M4A3 75 (W), the 1st Tank Battalion decided to retain

[7] The bulldog was adopted as the emblem of the Marine Corps in 1918.

Except for the vehicles completely destroyed on Peleliu, the 1st Tank Battalion kept its former M4A2s for Okinawa. The markings remained unchanged as can be seen here. Note the cream-colored stripe on the glacis and the gun barrel of these M4A2s from B Company. (NARA)

The M32B3 recovery vehicle was also given a number, as shown on this image. These vehicles were assigned to the company's maintenance section. (Corporal John F. Naut, USMCR via Michael J. Livingston)

Above: B Company set up a maintenance workshop in a village somewhere on Okinawa. Two post-Peleliu modifications are visible here: the commander's hatch is of a late model (as opposed to the early split-hatch model) and track links are now covering the vehicle's flanks. The latter is a battlefield modification in response to the growing number of antitank guns encountered during the Okinawa campaign. (USMC HD)

Right: Although effective, the additional steel track protection did not prevent the 47 mm rounds from penetrating the armor, as this image shows (turret). The A1 suspension was also protected by horizontal steel bars in order to prevent access to this vulnerable part of the tank. Note the pierced steel plate mounted on the hull hatch to protect it from explosives charges, a modification that was specific to A Company. (Corporal John F. Naut, USMCR via Michael J. Livingston)

Above: Initially the flanks of the M4A2s on Okinawa were protected by beach matting designed for crossing soft ground. They were to protect the flanks against magnetic mines and antitank grenades but after a few weeks, the crews realized that the biggest threat came from antitank guns. The beach matting was therefore replaced by track links. The pierced steel plate on the driver's hatch indicates this is an M4A2 from A Company. (NARA)

Below: This photo taken on Pavuvu shows the damage to A6 of 2nd Platoon, A Company. Two shells have penetrated the armor, the biggest coming from a 37 mm gun, whereas the smallest was probably caused by an antitank grenade fired from a rifle. The markings are clearly visible on the hull and turret. (Corporal John F. Naut, USMCR via Michael J. Livingston)

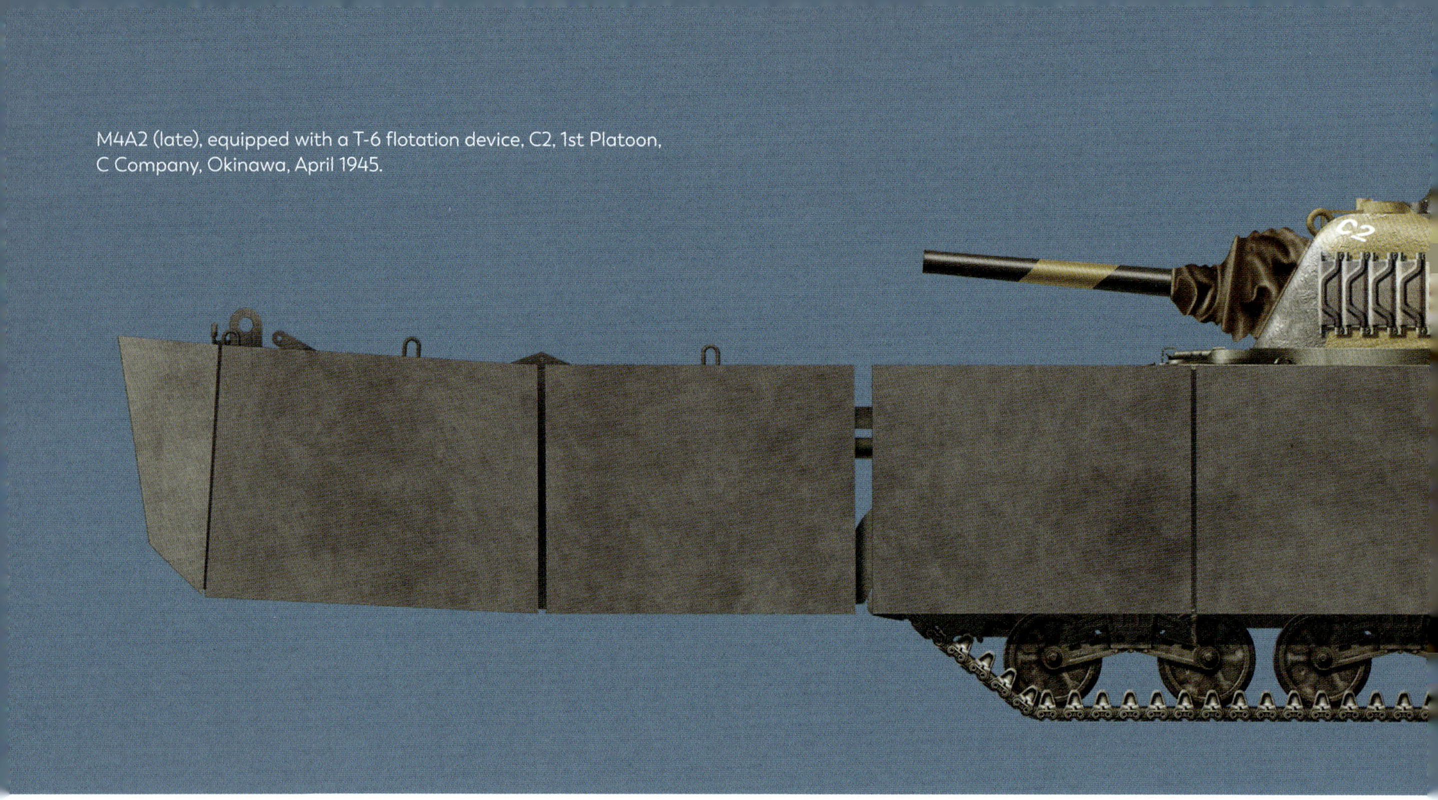

M4A2 (late), equipped with a T-6 flotation device, C2, 1st Platoon, C Company, Okinawa, April 1945.

Below: This tank from C Company on Okinawa has a two-tone camouflage scheme made of large splotches of sand-colored paint. This vehicle belonging to 1st Platoon is one of the six M4A2s to have been fitted with a flotation device (T-6) before the landing on Okinawa. (NARA via Ken Estes)

its M4A2s (most of which were in good condition since they had not been used on Peleliu), for Okinawa. During this campaign, all the companies from 1st Tank Battalion operated together for the first time since their activation in 1941.

On Okinawa, the battalion was equipped with 50 M4A2 Shermans, 15 per company (A, B, and C), a command tank, and four replacement tanks in the H&S Company. The three combat companies each received an M32B2 recovery vehicle.

Note that during the battle, 1st Tank Battalion received 39 replacement tanks, of which 17 were gasoline-engine M4A3 75 (W)s.[8] An M32B3 was also supplied. On Okinawa, the vehicles kept the tactical markings used on Peleliu.

On some Shermans, a camouflage scheme consisting of large dark (almost black) olive-drab patches and cream-colored stripes was applied over the factory-painted olive drab.

Tientsin, China (October 1945–January 1947)

When the 1st Marine Division was deployed in China with the survivors of the 1st Tank Battalion, the surviving M4A2s from the battle of Okinawa were entirely repainted forest green to make them look "new." The coding the vehicles used during the preceding campaigns was retained and applied again on the turrets. In 1946, the battalion obtained new M4A3s, some of which were fitted with a 105 mm cannon. The unit kept some of its M4A2s until the 1st Tank Battalion left China at the beginning of 1947.

[8] Mechanics and tank crews were not acquainted with the new gasoline engines.

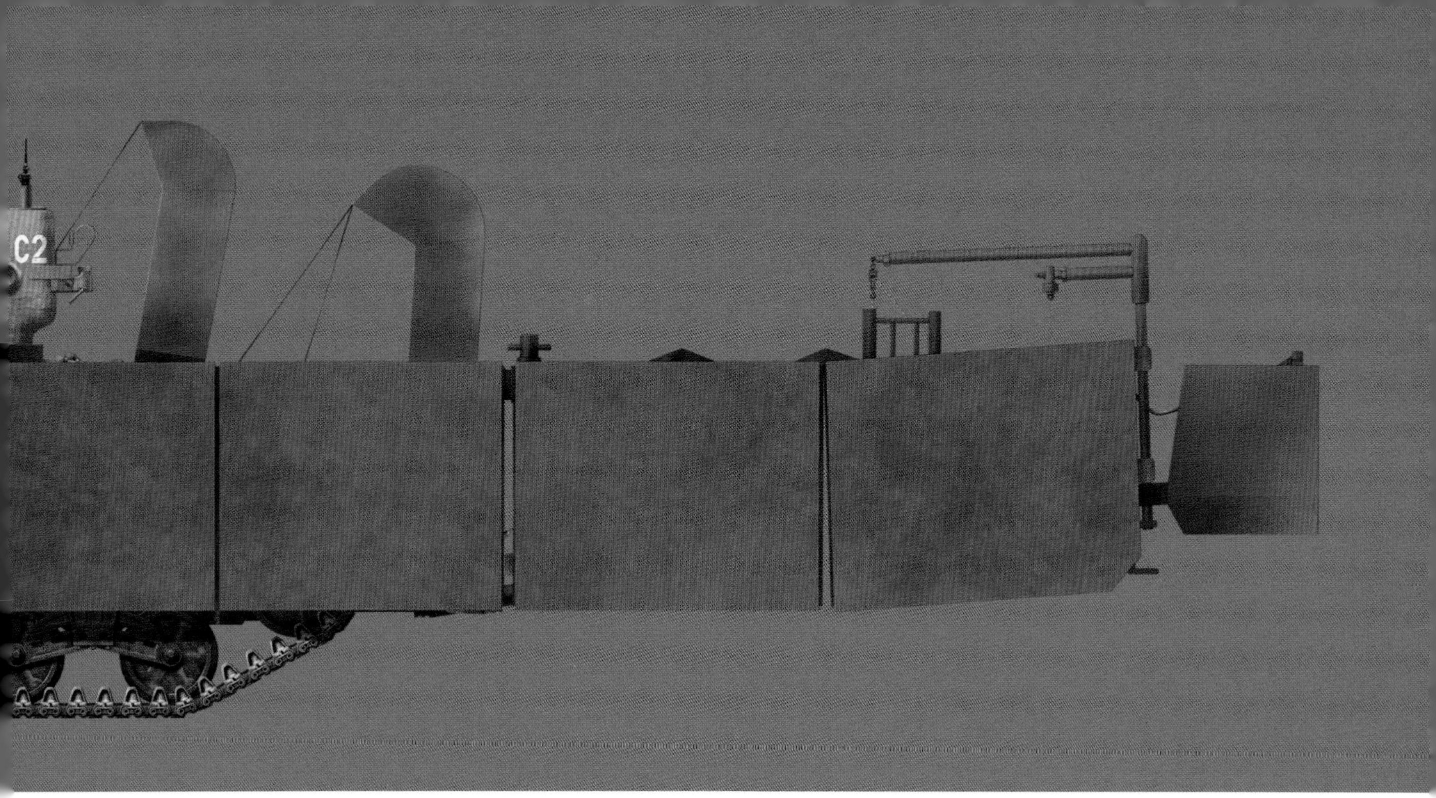

Some vehicles were given a name, not a very common practice within the 1st Tank Battalion. A9 was also given a bulldog's head as a mascot. These photos were taken in China between 1945 and 1947. (Corporal John F. Naut, USMCR via Michael J. Livingston)

Above: The 1st Tank Battalion was deployed at Tientsin in China for maintaining order after Japan surrendered in 1945. The M4A2s, of which some had served at Peleliu and Okinawa, were reconditioned. Here the additional armor made up of track links has been removed and the tank totally repainted. Note the rubber tracks to prevent damaging the roads when tanks are moving. The tactical markings remain unchanged. (Corporal John F. Naut, USMCR via Michael J. Livingston)

Right: The 1st Tank Battalion was the first USMC unit deployed overseas to receive the M4 Sherman armed with a 105 mm cannon. The vehicle in the foreground has the registration number 103106. (Corporal John F. Naut, USMCR via Michael J. Livingston)

2 The Defense Battalions' Tank Platoons

After the Japanese captured Wake Island in December 1941, the organization of the Defense Battalions[9] was changed. As the analysts had concluded that the presence of tanks would have delayed the Japanese long enough to allow American reinforcements to arrive, it was decided to incorporate a mobile armored unit in each of the 20 existing Defense Battalions.

Although they had been created for defense, the tank platoons of the 9th, 10th, and 11th Defense Battalions were used in an offensive, supporting U.S. Army divisions during the New Georgia campaign (July–August 1943). These Defense Battalion Tank Platoons were theoretically made up of five M3 or M3A1 tanks. The three tank units mobilized during the New Georgia campaign were, in reality, all overequipped, and included eight M3A1s each. The offensive nature of the conflict against Japan, the USMC's mechanized expansion, and in particular, the allocation of enough divisionary tank battalions, led to the Marine Corps' decision to disband these tank platoons in the fall of 1943.

[9] Deliberately, only the units that participated in active combat are dealt with here. In all, 20 Defense Battalions were activated and deployed in the Pacific for the defense of strategic islands.

An M3A1 from the Tank Platoon, 9th Defense Battalion, moving inland after landing on Rendora, in New Georgia. The tank is still equipped with its front fenders. These were quickly removed as the mud collected between the tracks and the fenders, hindering the vehicle's progress. (NARA)

Tank Platoon, 9th Defense Battalion

This unit was the only one to paint a black or cream-colored human skull on the sides of the tank turrets. Inside, a number was painted on the upper part of the skull; this was probably to indicate the position of the vehicle in the platoon. The most prominent markings on the M3A1 in this unit were the USMC numbers painted in big yellow figures on the hull flanks. These numbers, in the format USMC 60XXX, were used by the three units described here.

Tank Platoon, 10th Defense Battalion

As well as the USMC numbers painted on the hull flanks, a yellow disc was applied on the front vertical armor plate. The vehicle number was also painted yellow, between the hatches of the driver and co-driver's posts.

Tank Platoon, 11th Defense Battalion

The tank's USMC number and the yellow disc, identical to the one used by the 10th Defense Battalion, were also used by the 11th on its vehicles. Some M3A1s also had a name painted white on the turret sides, like *Patty* or *Baby Doll*. Several years after the war, tankman Hal Rogers remembers that one of the tanks was christened *Chief* and had a highly colored Native American painted on both flanks of the hull.

Above: This photo shows the symbol of the 9th Defense Battalion Tank Platoon: a black skull with the tank number on the forehead—here 6. The significance of the white paint which extends around the side observation slot of the turret remains unknown. (Ed Gilbert)

Right: Progressing through the jungle on muddy tracks put the mechanics and the personnel to the test. The towing cable became an indispensable tool and was kept available on all tanks. The yellow circle on the left of the hull indicates that this is a tank from the 10th or 11th Defense Battalion. (USMC HD)

Above: Some tanks had a name painted on the turret. Here *Patty*, an M3A1 from the 11th Defense Battalion Tank Platoon, is stuck in the mud on New Georgia in July 1943. (USMC HD)

Right: Sergeant Robert J. Miller posing proudly on his tank, called *Baby-Doll*, after the battle of Arundel Island. The vehicle belongs to the 11th Defense Battalion. Note that the Marine is wearing a civilian hat: before the war he had played in the Montgomery baseball team; hence the "M." (Oscar E. Gilbert)

Below: A column of Stuart tanks from the 11th Defense Battalion newly landed, heading for Munda aerodrome, to the southwest of New Georgia Island. Being the main objective of this campaign, the aerodrome was attacked by elements of three tank platoons from the 9th, 10th, and 11th Defense Battalions. (NARA via Ed Gilbert)

M3A1, No. 6, Tank Platoon, 9th Defense Battalion, New Georgia, July 1943.

Below left: The command tank of 1st Lieutenant Robert Blake (in the turret) in the New Georgia jungle in 1943. Blake commanded the Tank Platoon of the 9th Defense Battalion for the whole campaign. Starting with eight tanks, he ended up with a single operational vehicle. (NARA)

Below right: A diesel M3A1 of the 10th Defense Battalion and its crew, posing on Banika in the Solomon Islands before embarking for New Georgia. Note the yellow circle on the left as well as the vehicle number painted between the driver and assistant driver's positions. (NARA)

3

The 1st Corps Tank Battalion (Medium)

The 1st Corps Tank Battalion (medium) was activated in January 1943. It was made up of four companies of Sherman medium tanks, each being "loaned" to one of the USMC divisions then in existence.[10]

The aim was to reinforce the standard armored allocation of a division, since the divisional tank battalions were only equipped with light Stuart tanks.

B Company should have been deployed at Bougainville in November 1943 but the dense jungle, the thick mud, and the lack of infrastructure enabling 30-ton tanks to move around, made this deployment abort.

Finally, only C Company was deployed to support the 2nd Marine Division during the battle of Tarawa in November 1943.

Just like the Defense Battalion Tank Platoons (preceding chapter), the 1st Corps Tank Battalion (medium) was no longer of any use within the Marine Corps whose ranks were being mechanized very quickly. It was disbanded on February 13, 1944, after existing for a year.

The Markings

The naming system for the tanks in the battalion was standardized and followed the rule of using the company's letter (A, B, C, or D) as the name's initial.

These names were at first painted on the instruction M4A2s at Camp Pendleton. Before being deployed in the Pacific, new M4A2s were

10 The 5th and 6th divisions were only activated in 1944.

This photo of a training M4A2 from C Company, 1st Corps Tank Battalion (medium), was taken at Camp Pendleton (United States) in 1943. The tank's name was painted yellow on the hull flanks. The U.S. Army registration number is still visible on the rear. The battalion insignia has not appeared yet; it was painted on the vehicles in New Caledonia, mid-1943. (Ed Gazel)

Taken in January 1944, this photo shows B Company, 1st Corps Tank Battalion (medium)'s tank park in New Caledonia after a hurricane had passed. Not all the tanks have been given a name, as the M4A2 in the center shows. However, the battalion's symbol, an elephant, is clearly visible. Note the registration number using the USMC format, partly hidden behind the wooden pole. C Company, deployed at Tarawa a few months earlier, had no USMC registration numbers. (NARA)

obtained and the names were applied to these new vehicles when the battalion arrived in New Caledonia in August 1943.

Except for those of C Company, most tank names have been lost to time. Only *Butch* and *Brat* in B Company and *Dood-it* in D Company are known. The identity of the 14 Shermans in C Company, which took part in the battle of Tarawa, was found thanks to a study published in 2015 and based on an analysis of the photos and the eyewitness accounts of the unit's last veterans.[11]

Names of C Company tanks, 1st Corps Tank Battalion			
HQ Platoon	1st Platoon	2nd Platoon	3rd Platoon
Cecilia	*Chicago*	*Cobra*	*Cannonball*
Commando	*China Gal*	*Clipper*	*Colorado*
*Cherokee**	*Cherry*	*Cuddles*	*Condor*
	The Count	*Conga*	*Charlie*

* An M32B2 recovery vehicle was attached to the HQ Platoon. The lack of experience in the loading of ships and the lack of space caused C Company to leave the M32B2 in New Caledonia.

[11] The study was published in the book *Tanks in Hell, a Marine Corps Tank Company on Tarawa* (Casemate, 2015). *Cf* Bibliography.

This image of the M4A2 *Colorado* from the 3rd Platoon, C Company, was taken on Red Beach 3 at Tarawa on November 20, 1943. The tank was deliberately parked on the edge of the shore to avoid driving over the Marines all huddled up on the beach. Its name and the elephant were painted yellow on the hull flank. (USMC HD)

Above: The name *Condor* was suggested by the tank's driver, Corporal Raymond A. Barker and approved by the rest of the crew. The former U.S. Army registration number (3035025) is still legible next to the elephant. The name *Mike* has been painted white above the bow machine gun, but the reason for this is not known. (USMC HD)

Below left: The wreck of *Cannonball* on Tarawa, the command tank of 3rd Platoon. The U.S. Army format registration number 3035028 painted light blue is visible on the flank. However, the name and the battalion insignia seemed to have been hidden under a layer of paint. Barely visible is the white star painted on the turret when the tank came out of the factory. (USMC HD)

Below right: *Charlie* was another M4A2 from the 3rd Platoon. Several tanks in the unit were equipped with racks holding eight 5-gallon cans of water on the rear. *Charlie* was put out of action by several 75 mm Type 88 cannon shots. It was recovered with five other M4A2s from C Company, rebuilt, and given to the 2nd Separate Tank Company, which used it at Eniwetok in 1944. (USMC HD)

Above: This slightly blurred photo shows *Cherry*, a tank from the 1st Platoon after the battle. The M4A2 had sunk into a shell hole off Red Beach 1 on November 20. Note the five-point star painted on the turret. (NARA)

Below: This photo was taken on November 23, in the afternoon, and shows the tankmen of the 1st Corps Tank Battalion (medium) recovering the wrecks from around the island. *Colorado* is in front of *Chicago*, which had drowned its engine in a shell hole on the morning of November 20. *Chicago* was the platoon leader's tank of the 1st Platoon. (NARA)

As well as having names, the tanks were numbered from 1–14:

- Numbers 1 and 2 were respectively for the company commander and his executive officer.
- Numbers 3–6, 7–10, and 11–14 applied respectively to the 1st, 2nd, and 3rd Platoons. These numbers were not, however, painted on the vehicle and were used only for the radio call sign.

While the battalion was stationed in New Caledonia, a Marine—who remains unidentified—designed the unit's insignia: an elephant with a red blanket on its back; it has lifted one of its feet and a cloud of dust is blowing from its trunk.

The color of the elephant (and the tank's name) was usually yellow. In some cases, the elephant and the name were painted gray. Sometimes, crews combined the colors. For example, *Commando* (C Company) had a gray elephant and a yellow name for the tank.

On the black-and-white photos, the different shades of gray enable one to distinguish whether the elephant was yellow (a darker shade than the dust cloud) or gray (a similar shade to the dust cloud).

All the tanks supplied before the departure for New Caledonia had white five-point stars on the sides and the rear of the turret. In the case of C Company, the stars were covered with a thick layer of khaki-green paint before landing on Tarawa.

Some vehicles in the battalion seemed to have been given USMC numbers while the unit was stationed in New Caledonia. These numbers were probably attributed after C Company left for Tarawa, since none of the M4A2s in this company had these markings. Several Shermans still had the former U.S. Army registration numbers painted blue on the sides of the hull.

Except for C Company, the battalion vehicles were not used in combat and were in excellent condition at the beginning of 1944, at the time the unit was disbanded. Although at this precise moment, factory production was in full swing, the process of shipping tanks to USMC fighting units in the Pacific was still very slow.

Thus, the fact that these M4A2s were present in the South Pacific at the beginning of 1944 explains why the USMC chose to use these companies (tanks and personnel) to reorganize the 3rd Tank Battalion, at the time only equipped with M3A1 light tanks. As most of the crews had remained in the 3rd Tank Battalion, the markings and, in particular, the elephant—the symbol of the 1st Corps Tank Battalion (medium)—was still in use in 1944 and 1945.

China Gal also belonged to the 1st Platoon. The tank's name was chosen by the crew and referred to the name of a San Diego dancer. The vehicle was taken over by the company commander, 1st Lieutenant Edward L. Bale (standing, in the center) after his own tank had lost the use of its gun in a duel with a Japanese Type 95 tank on D-Day. (USMC HD)

Right: *Conga* belonged to the 2nd Platoon. It was put out of action by friendly mortar fire on November 21, 1943. Several other M4A2s, as well as some M3A1s from the 2nd Tank Battalion, are waiting to be recovered and scrapped after the battle. (Kim T. Harrison)

Below: A photo of the wreck of *Cecilia* taken on Tarawa. The tank's name and the elephant have been masked by a thick layer of paint before the battle for obscure reasons. The tank was named after the newborn daughter of the tank's driver, Alfonso A. Chavez. (NARA)

M4 TANKS OF THE 1ST CORPS TANK BATTALION, 1940–1941

M4A2, *Colorado*, 3rd Platoon, C Company, November 20, 1943, on Tarawa.

M4A2 (mid-production), No. 2, *Commando*, HQ Platoon, C Company, Tarawa, November 1943.

4 The 2nd Tank Battalion

Just like the 1st Tank Battalion, the 2nd was gradually activated from May 1, 1941. Its A Company was in fact just another name for the 4th Tank Company.

Company B of 2nd Tank Battalion was the first tank unit to be deployed overseas after the United States' entry into the war. An M3 is pictured here on the docks of Pago-Pago in the Samoa Islands in 1942. It bears the number B1 (1st Platoon) painted yellow on the turret sides. The five-point star can be seen on the hull and turret. (NARA via Ken Estes)

While the other companies had not yet been activated, A Company was assigned to the 6th Marines and deployed in Iceland from July 1941 to March 1942. Iceland was occupied by British and American troops to prevent this strategic island from falling into German hands.

Companies B to E, formed between September 1941 and February 1942, were then deployed one after the other in the South Pacific from January onwards.

On August 8, 1942, two C Company M3 tanks and their crews were attached to the 2nd Marines in order to take part in the capture of the Island of Tanambogo, to the north of Guadalcanal. Subsequently, B Company took part in the fighting for Guadalcanal from November 1942 to February 1943. The battalion fought as a whole for the first time during the summer of 1944, in the Mariana Islands (Saipan and Tinian) supporting the 2nd Marine Division.

Finally, the battalion took part in the Okinawa campaign as a reserve but only A Company, supporting the 8th Marines, landed on the islands of Iheya, Aguni, and Okinawa in April and June 1945.

The 2nd Tank Battalion was part of the Army of Occupation in Japan, based in Nagasaki from September 1945 to January 1946. It returned to the United States in February 1946.

The 2nd Tank Battalion was thus the first American tank unit to be deployed overseas (Iceland, July 1941), the first USMC tank unit to be deployed after the United States entered the war (B Company, Samoa Islands, January 1942), the first USMC tank unit to engage the enemy (C Company, Tanambogo, August 8, 1942), and the last American tank unit to be deployed in combat during World War II (A Company, Okinawa, June 15–22, 1945).

First Deployments (1942)

According to some photographs and interviews with veterans, 2nd Tank Battalion companies followed the letter–number code system to identify their M3 tanks. This was probably inspired by the then common practice within the U.S. Army.

The letters indicated the company (A–E), and the number (1–18) was the position of the tank within the unit. The sequence 1–5 was reserved for 1st

Platoon, 6–10 for the 2nd, and 11–15 for the 3rd. Numbers 16–18 were reserved for the HQ Platoon. The system was harmonized within the battalion.

When the code was painted, this was on the tank's turret sides. However, the letter–number code system does not seem to have been systematically painted.

Marine Ernest L. Adams imagined and painted a mascot for C Company: a bulldog, wearing armor and a helmet, standing in front of the Company's letter. The mascot seems to have been accepted (or tolerated) by the company commander since "Mac the Bulldog" was painted on the tank hulls.

The mascot does not seem to have survived the unit's deployment in the Solomon Islands.

Right: Mac the Bulldog was C Company's insignia. Imagined and painted by Marine Ernest Adams, he was generally represented standing placed next to the company letter. According to witnesses, several versions of the warlike bulldog existed, among which was one wearing a tanker helmet. (Interpretation by artist Candice Pangaud, acrylic on paper, 2022)

Right: This photo shows an M3 from C Company stationed in the Fijis before the Tulagi–Guadalcanal campaign. A white stripe surrounds the turret and a white star has been painted on the side hatch. The name *Chief* and Mac the Bulldog, the company symbol, have been painted on the hull. No number is visible. (Benjamin Pugsley via Ken Estes)

Below: Although it did not theoretically have any tanks, E Company of the 2nd Tank Battalion did in fact have a few M3s, and even a pair of Marmon-Herrington tankettes. This photo, taken in New Zealand, shows Tank No. 4 being fully serviced. Below the tactical marking, the crew has painted the tank's serial number (1173). On the side of the turret, a T for "Tanks" has been painted inside a triangle, the symbol of the Division Special Troops, to which the tanks were assigned until 1944. (NARA)

Left: The wreck of Tank No. 14 from 3rd Platoon, C Company, on the Island of Tanambogo after the fighting in 1942. This was the first USMC tank to be put out of action by the enemy during the war. Unlike the photo taken in the Fijis, this M3 does not show any particular markings. The unit either obtained new vehicles before the campaign or repainted its tanks before they were deployed in the Solomon Islands. (Author's Collection)

Below: An M3 hybrid from D Company during maneuvers at the end of 1942–beginning of 1943. Although the tactical markings were similar to those used in 1944, they had a different significance. Here, D-11 indicates the 11th tank of D Company belonging to 3rd Platoon. The markings were painted white, whereas the USMC registration number was painted yellow. (NARA)

Right: In C Company, the crews painted the name of the tank in white on the side of the hull. It began with the company letter, like here with *Columbus* which belonged to 2nd Platoon, as indicated by the triangle's position (pointing downwards) of the Special Troops. (USMC HD)

Below: The 2nd Tank Battalion tank park was set up in an aircraft shelter on the island of Betio in Tarawa Atoll. The vehicles belong to the three platoons of C Company, as the varied direction of the triangles on the turrets of these M3A1s indicates. (NARA)

Above left: B Company invented a clever identification system: the vehicles had two numbers painted inside a triangle. The first indicated the platoon and the second the tank's position in the platoon. Here we can see the white triangle painted on the left-hand side of Tank No. 25's turret. The "2," as well as the triangle's position, indicates that the vehicle belonged to 2nd Platoon. (USMC HD)

Above right: This photo shows M3A1 No. 11 from 3rd Platoon, C Company (left) and *Conqueror* (right) whose platoon is unknown. We can guess at the five-point star on the turret of No. 11, a current practice in this company. (NARA)

Below: M3A1 *Boogie Woogie* No. 33 belonged to 3rd Platoon, B Company. Unlike C Company, B Company tended to paint the name of its tanks on the turret. Here, however, it seems to have been painted on the right-hand side only. (NARA)

Tarawa (November 1943)

The 2nd Tank Battalion companies were reequipped with diesel M3A1s for the assault on Tarawa. A new marking system was devised: an isosceles triangle with a number inside it, painted white on the turret sides, and sometimes at the rear of the turret and the tank hull. The triangle was the official symbol of the Division Special Troops—the units placed under the direct control of the Division Headquarters.

The platoon was designated by the triangle's direction. A triangle pointing upwards indicated the 1st Platoon, pointing downwards, the 2nd Platoon, and pointing sideways, the 3rd Platoon. Before Tarawa, it was decided to break down the HQ Platoon: each of the three tanks from the platoon reinforced the line platoons, thus forming "reinforced platoons" consisting of six tanks instead of five.

Only B and C Companies, equipped with 18 tanks each, were deployed on Tarawa.[12] They were different from each other, notably in their system of vehicle numbering. In B Company, the numbering system was new for the time. Made up of two digits, the number was painted black on the solid white triangle. The first figure indicated the platoon (1, 2, and 3), the second indicated the position of the tank in the platoon: from 0 to 5.

According to Marine Arthur Russell, the idea behind a code consisting of two numbers was to give the illusion of a powerful armored force. "If the enemy had seen that [number], they could think that there would be 20 or 30 tanks while there was only six or seven."

A name starting with the company call sign was also painted on the turret. The names *Burp* and *Boogie Woogie* have been identified.

C Company used a more standard system for the time. The tanks were numbered 1–18, with the numbers 1–5 for 1st Platoon, 6–10 for the 2nd, and 11–15 for the 3rd. The tanks in the HQ Platoon were numbered 16, 17, and 18 respectively assigned to the 1st, 2nd, and 3rd Platoons.

The triangle (empty) with white sides was painted on the turret (sides and rear) and sometimes on the tank hull. The tank number was painted white inside the triangle. The names started with the letter C and were painted in white on the hull sides.

This photo was taken on Green Beach. Two tanks from B Company are visible: No. 30 (3rd Platoon commander) on the right and No. 11 from 1st Platoon. The latter has been put out of action by a shot to the right sprocket. The tank has obviously been towed here while waiting to be repaired. (USMC HD)

[12] The D (Scouts) and H&S (HQ) Companies were also deployed on Tarawa, but they had no tanks.

The calligraphy and size of the letters were not standard and varied from one platoon to another. The 1st Platoon had christened its tanks with the names of Native American tribes: *Cherokee*, *Chief*, *Cheyenne*, *Chippewa*, *Choctaw*, and *Comanche*. On the tops of the C Company tanks, there was also a white five-point star for aerial identification. Note that B Company's 3rd Platoon had its triangle directed systematically towards the rear of the vehicle, whereas C Company rotated it through 90 degrees to the right. Thus, on the right-hand side of the turret, the triangle pointed to the rear, whereas on the left-hand side, it pointed to the front.

The Marianas (June–August 1944)

For this campaign, the 2nd Tank Battalion was reorganized in three tank companies comprising 15 M4A2s each (including a tankdozer), plus a M32B2 recovery vehicle

Having learnt the lessons of Tarawa, the Marines modified M3A1 tanks into flamethrowers. Dubbed "Satans" by the crews, they allowed the flamethrower user to get closer to the Japanese pillboxes, protected by the tank's armor. Though no plan was made for them in the Tank Battalions' new organization, the Satan tanks were put all together in unofficial D Companies. M5A1 reinforced them as command tanks. The 4th Tank Battalion adopted a similar organization for the Mariana campaign. Once again, the identification system of the 2nd Tank Battalions was modified so that it was standardized for all the companies.

A hybrid system somewhere between both of those used earlier—a letter-number code—was used to which a name was added. The letter corresponded to the company's letter (A, B, C, or D) and the number followed the logic used for the first time on Tarawa by B Company. The first number indicated the platoon and the second, the vehicle's position in the platoon.

Thus, tank number A-30 corresponded to the platoon leader of 3rd Platoon, A Company.

Given that the smallest combat group utilized corresponded to the section made up of two tanks, the platoon leader (B-20, for example) worked with B-21, and B-22 with B-23. In this second configuration, the section was commanded by the platoon sergeant.

Whether it was M4A2 Shermans (A, B, and C Companies) or M3A1 Satans or M5A1s (D Company), the tactical markings were painted white on the sides and the rear of the turret, as well as on the fording kit at the rear of the tank.

Left: After Tarawa, the 2nd Tank Battalion standardized a more elaborate tactical marking system. Inspired by the system used by B Company at Tarawa, it was completed by adding a prefix: the letter designating the company. The simple and effective system enabled this M3A1 Satan to be attributed immediately to 1st Platoon, D Company. It is the vehicle belonging to the platoon commander, as indicated by the zero at the end of the code. Note the aerial recognition star on the turret roof, a marking standardized throughout the whole battalion. (NARA)

M3 AND M4 TANKS OF THE 2ND TANK BATTALION, 1943–1944

M3A1, No. 33, *Boogie Woogie*, 3rd Platoon, B Company, Tarawa, November 1943.

M3A1, No. 2, *Chippewa*, 1st Platoon, C Company, Tarawa, November 1943.

M4A2 (mid-production), B-22, *Buffalo*, 2nd Platoon, B Company, Saipan, June 1944.

Above: This late model M4A2 belonged to Lieutenant Merle Severns, commanding the 3rd Platoon of C Company. As well as the tactical marking, each vehicle bore a name which also began with the company's call sign. Here C.O.D has a double meaning: *Come On Darling* or *Cash On Delivery*. A pin-up seems to have been painted under the tank's name. (NARA)

Below: As well as the tactical markings, B Company painted a simplified emblem of the USMC on its tanks with a stencil: a globe surmounted by an eagle together with a ship's anchor. The hull markings were painted yellow, whereas the code on the turret was white. (NARA)

Left: C Company's tankdozer on Saipan. This company was special in that it was made up of a mix of late model (as here) and mid-production M4A2s. This tank had no name. (NARA)

Below: A photograph of D-21 *Dusty* on Saipan. This is one of the 11 Stuarts converted into flamethrowers and used by the 2nd Tank Battalion. The conversion consisted of replacing the 37 mm cannon of an M3A1 with a Canadian Ronson M3A1 flamethrower. The inside of the vehicle was redesigned in order to house the gas tanks for the flamethrower (napalm was not yet in use), and compressed CO_2. (NARA)

Tank markings of the 2nd Tank Battalion, Mariana campaign, summer of 1944				
	HQ Platoon	1st Platoon	2nd Platoon	3rd Platoon
A Company (M4A2) NB: The name *Angel* existed but its tactical number is not known	A-40 A-41 A-42 M32B2	A-10 *Ace* A-11 A-12 A-13 *Amok*	A-20 *Awol* A-21 *Acorn* A-22 *Amen* A-23 *Allah*	A-30 *Amapola* A-31 A-32 *Ashland* A-33 *Apache*
B Company (M4A2) NB: The name *Billie Blue* existed but its tactical number is not known	B-40 *Betio* B-41 *Bastard* B-42 M32B2	B-10 *Bubbles* B-11 *Bonnie* B-12 *Bonita* B-13 *Betty*	B-20 *Beast* B-21 B-22 *Buffalo* B-23 *Bruin* (?)	B-30 *Bozo* B-31 *Butch* B-32 B-33 *Bosco*
C Company (M4A2)	C-40 *Caesar* C-41 *Can-Do* C-42 *unnamed* M32B2	C-10 C-11 C-12 C-13 *Cavalier*	C-20 C-21 *Corker* C-22 *Comet* C-23	C-30 *C.O.D.* C-31 *Check-It* C-32 C-33 *Clipper*
D Company (2xM5A1 11xM3A1 Satan) *M5A1 identified	D-40*	D-10 D-11 *Defense* D-12 *Dudley* D-13 *Dope*	D-20 D-21 *Dusty* D-22 D-23	D-30 D-31 *Dong* D-32 *Denkum* D-33 *Defy*

The name of the tank was painted yellow and began with the company letter (A, B, C, and D). It was reproduced in capital letters on the side hull armor plates.

The table above gives examples of the tactical markings associated with the names, as used by the 2nd Tank Battalion at Saipan and Tinian.

B Company also painted the Marine Corps' simplified symbol below the tank's name, on the center of the glacis, and on the rear of the fording kit, below the tactical marking. Several crews also painted pin-ups on the side or the front of their tanks.

Finally, five-point stars were painted white on the top of the turrets of all the battalion's tanks for aerial observers to identify the front line.

The crew of the M4A2 A-21 *Acorn* posing for a souvenir photo after several weeks of fighting. The name was painted yellow and the turret tactical marking was white. (Dona Pearson-Werner)

Left and below: *Amapola* was the title of a popular song in the 1940s. The name was chosen by the crew following its proposal by Private Joe Woolum, the gunner, as a tribute to a childhood friend who used to sing the song regularly. The turret marking, painted white, could be seen at a great distance, unlike the name painted yellow. This Sherman was temporarily put out of action in the final days of the battle of Saipan after driving over a mine. (NARA)

Above: As with the Sherman medium tanks, the Stuarts had their tactical number painted on the rear of the turret. Two M3A1 Satans from 1st Platoon, D Company, were hastily camouflaged on Saipan, summer 1944. (NARA)

Right: Another example of markings with *Clipper* from C Company on Saipan. This is a mid-production M4A2, as shown by the driver and assistant driver's positions, which stick up over the glacis. (NARA)

The command tank of B Company bears the tactical number B-40, and was named *Betio* by its crew. (NARA)

A-20 *Awol* had all the specific markings of the 2nd Tank Battalion during the Mariana campaign in 1944. All the tanks in the battalion were painted olive drab. (NARA)

D-33 *Defy* belonged to 3rd Platoon, D Company. The Satan tanks were directly adapted from the lessons learnt in the fighting on Tarawa in 1943. In addition to the 11 flamethrower tanks, D Company also had two command M5A1s. (NARA)

Rear view of the M4A2 B32 on Saipan. We can see the tactical marking on the bottom of the fording kit, under which there is the USMC emblem. (Arthur J. Strenge Jr. via A. Figallo)

Left: Most of the tanks in the 2nd Tank Battalion were used again for the battle of Tinian. Here we see the M4A2 C22 *Comet* from 2nd Platoon, C Company, operating in support of a 2nd Marine Division unit in a sugarcane field. (NARA)

Below: This Sherman is the company command vehicle, as indicated by the turret tactical marking. (NARA)

Above: After Saipan was captured, the 2nd Tank Battalion received several tanks from the Hawaii depots to replace the vehicles lost in combat. C30, for example, was abandoned after running over a mine and was replaced by a new vehicle before landing on Tinian. The initial name was *C.O.D.* but was changed to *Chubby*, referring to the tank commander's chubbiness. (NARA)

Right: D-31 *Dong* coming to the help of a jeep which flooded its engine during the landing on Tinian in July 1944. Note that the name of the tank has been painted above the USMC registration number. USMC emblems painted yellow are also visible on the flank of the hull. (NARA)

On Tinian, the 2nd Marine Division was detached to the 4th Marine Division which commanded the operations. We can see here the application of this attachment, with tanks from C Company, 2nd Tank Battalion (C11 and C42 on the right) in direct support of M4A2s from B Company of the 4th Tank Battalion, on the left. (NARA)

The Okinawa Campaign (April–June 1945)

The battalion organization was revised before the Okinawa campaign. This time, the platoons were reduced to three tanks and an extra platoon was activated so as to maintain a total of 15 tanks in the company. This new organization was supposed to make command and control of the platoon easier.

Although the Marine Corps was transitioning to the M4A3 (75) Ws, the 2nd Tank Battalion succeeded in obtaining some late production M4A2s, undoubtedly from among the last to be built.

Having proved their effectiveness, the tactical markings used during the Mariana campaign were

B10 *Boots* took part in the demonstration landing to the south of Okinawa on April 1, 1945, but was not landed. Note the series of rivets on the flanks of the hull: the flanks of all the M4s in the battalion were covered with additional steel plates to protect them from antitank shells. (USMC HD and USC)

M3 AND M4 TANKS OF THE 2ND TANK BATTALION, 1943–1944

M3A1 Satan, D-13, *Dope*, 1st Platoon, D Company, Saipan, July 1944.

M4A2 (late), A-40, *Attack*, 4th Platoon, A Company, Aguni, April 1945.

M4 TANK OF THE 2ND TANK BATTALION, 1944–1945

M4A2 (late), A-11, *Amapola*, 1st Platoon, A Company, Okinawa, June 1945.

A Company from the 2nd Tank Battalion operated in direct support of the 8th Marines on Okinawa. It was the only unit of the battalion to take part in the fighting on the island. The crew of the *Amapola* was reassigned to a new platoon after the Mariana campaign, as is indicated by the tactical marking on the turret. The tank has a multicolored camouflage scheme. (Critical Past)

re-used for Okinawa. A few slight modifications were applied, such as the size of the letters and numbers, which were enlarged so they could be read at a greater distance.

The five-point star was again painted on the roof of the turrets. A tankman from B Company, who had taken part in the demonstration landing to the south of Okinawa, commented: "We all hoped and prayed they [the Kamikaze aviators] didn't want to dive into us, as the big white star on top our five tanks were very good advertisement to the pilot that could easily dive his plane into our ship for the honor of his country."

Given the new structure of the companies, the code system was adapted so as to absorb a fifth platoon. Thus, the series -50 identified the HQ platoon with 50 for the company commander, 51 for the executive officer, and 52 for the tankdozer. The series -40, -30, -20, and -10 identified respectively the 4th, 3rd, 2nd, and 1st Platoons.

In A Company, tanks A-11 *Amapola*, A-40 *Attack*, and A-42 *Attain* have been identified and took part in the battles of Iheya, Aguni, and Okinawa.

5 The 3rd Tank Battalion

The 3rd Tank Battalion was formed in July 1942 on the sites of New River in North Carolina (East Coast of the United States) and of Camp Elliott in California (West Coast).

The battalion was regrouped in New Zealand in the spring of 1943 and took part in the Bougainville campaign from November onwards. It was then made up of three companies of 18 M3A1 tanks each. In March 1944, A Company was attached to the 4th Marines for taking Emirau. After the island was captured, the 4th Marines remained an independent regiment and A Company was definitively detached from the 3rd Tank Battalion to become the Tank Company, 4th Marines (see Chapter 6). At the same time, the 3rd Tank Battalion was reorganized and incorporated elements of the 1st Corps Tank Battalion (medium). The three companies were therefore reequipped with M4A2 Shermans.

The unit took part in the battles of Guam during the summer of 1944 and Iwo Jima at the beginning of 1945, where it retained its old M4A2s. After Japan

A section of M3A1 tanks from B Company is photographed being resupplied on Bougainville. The pale-green squares on the turret sides indicate that the vehicles belong to the 1st Platoon. (USMC HD)

surrendered, the battalion returned to the United States in December 1945 where it was disbanded the following month.

Bougainville (November 1943) and Emirau (March 1944)

Very early on, the 3rd Tank Battalion used geometric shapes to identify its platoons, a system inspired by that used in the U.S. Army at the end of World War I.

The battalion thus designated the 1st, 2nd, and 3rd Platoons by the shapes: square, circle, and diamond respectively. The HQ Platoon was probably identified by a triangle, but no source confirms this.

Large geometric shapes were painted on the sides and the rear of the turrets of the Stuarts from A Company. The numbers from 1–5 indicated the tank's position within the platoon.

Although the markings were traditionally painted yellow, the 1st Platoon was special in that it used lively colors: a white square with red sides with a red number. The five tanks of the 1st Platoon had a name painted white on both sides of the hull.

Square 1 was called *Nick's Nightmare*; Square 2 *Blood and Guts*; Square 3 *Pain in the Ass*; Square 4 *Death, Hell and Destruction*, and Square 5 *The Pay Off*. A pin-up was also painted on a single side of the hull.

Note that the vehicles' hulls were covered with thick canvas in order to prevent magnetic mines from sticking. This canvas was painted and the markings applied over them. They were only used at Bougainville: they were effective but tended to tear off when in contact with the vegetation.

B and C Companies used smaller numbers on the Stuarts' sides and rear of the turret. The shape size was too small to contain the tank number which was painted on the rear right or left of the turret.

C Company seems to have been the only unit to use the UNIS[13] marking system on Bougainville.

[13] The Unit Numerical Identification system (UNIS) was a code system theoretically used by each USMC division. It associated a geometric shape which identified the division with a series of three figures painted on the inside, unique to each unit. The succession of numbers for the same unit branch, the tanks for example, was specific to each division. Each branch of a division theoretically used the UNIS. In reality, only the 3rd and 4th Marine Divisions used it on a large scale.

Below left: This photograph enables us to make a comparison between the imposing size of an LVT-1 and that of the Stuart M3A1 tank supplied to most of the armored units of the USMC in 1943. It probably belongs to B Company. (NARA)

Below right: Square 1 from A Company had imposing and brightly colored white and red markings on the turret. This was the command tank of the 1st Platoon. Its vertical flanks are covered by canvas in order to protect it from magnetic mines. (NARA)

Above: This photo taken from a color film from 1943 shows Square 5 *The Pay Off*, from A Company on Bougainville. The prominent marking on the turret painted red and white is clearly visible here. Note the mud thrown up onto the glacis. (USMC HD and USC)

Below left: As well as the geometric shape (here hidden by the leg of the Marine sitting on the turret), a number was painted on the rear left or right of the turret in the case of B and C Companies. This is one of B Company's tanks. (NARA)

Below right: The 2nd Platoon (Circle Platoon) from B Company waiting for orders on the side of a track on Bougainville. On the closest vehicle (left) we can see the circle painted on the rear hatch of the turret as well as the number 5, painted next to the antiaircraft mount. (NARA)

Above: Another example of an A Company vehicle with its very visible markings. The tank's name and pin-up are painted on the canvas which has been stuck onto the tank to insulate it from magnetic mines. (NARA)

Below: A Company was detached so it could take part in the attack on the island of Emirau at the beginning of 1944 to support the 4th Marines. We can see here Diamond 1 of the 3rd Platoon (platoon leader's tank) being towed onto dry land. Note the marking, UNIS 632, on the jerrycan painted inside the flattened diamond. The geometrical shape indicates the 3rd Marine Division, the 6 designates the Special Troops, the 3 for the Tank Battalion, and the 2 for A Company. (NARA)

It was a flattened diamond with the number 634 painted inside. The diamond was the symbol of 3rd Marine Division; 6 designated the Special troops;[14] 3, the Tank Battalion; and 4, C Company.

Guam (July–August 1944)

Just before the Guam campaign, the 3rd Tank Battalion was reequipped with M4A2s and personnel from the former 1st Corps Tank Battalion (medium).

A Company inherited the personnel and the vehicles of A Company of the 1st Corps Tank Battalion; B Company inherited only the vehicles of its B Company; C Company inherited vehicles

[14] As indicated previously, before the fall of 1944, the tanks belonged to the Special Troops, under the control of the divisional HQ. After Guadalcanal, they were very quickly put under the command of the (infantry) regiments where their use was more appropriate in terms of direct support. In the fall of 1944, the tank battalion became a semi-autonomous entity in the division, in the same way as the artillery for example.

and personnel of the former D Company of the 1st Corps.

Thus, the 3rd Tank Battalion adopted the insignia of the former 1st Corps Tank Battalion (medium): an elephant, which was kept on most of the vehicles fighting on Guam.

This insignia was the only similarity between the three companies' marking systems. Indeed, each set up its own system of tactical identification independently of the other two.

A Company's tanks were thus given names beginning with the letter A—*Andrea*, *Atlas*, *Arsenic*, or *Angel*, for example. The name was painted on the sides of the hull, under the elephant. A winged five-point star (like the planes) was painted on the rear of the turret. A similar star was painted on the turret roofs for aerial identification.

The tanks were numbered 1–14 with numbers 1–4 for the 1st Platoon; 5–8 for the 2nd; 9–12 for the 3rd; 13–14 for the HQ Section.[15] The tank number was painted white on the lower rear part of the fording kit. The USMC registration number was also visible on several vehicles. B Company kept the system of geometric shapes used at Bougainville. They were painted white with the tank number inside them and were applied on the turret (sides and rear) and on the rear of the tank (hull and fording kit).[16] The 1st, 2nd, and 3rd platoons were identified by a square, a circle, and a diamond respectively, whereas the HQ Platoon was identified by a triangle.

Above: Tanks and infantrymen from the 3rd Marine Division advancing in the jungle on Guam in the summer of 1944. It is a platoon of M4A2s from A Company. The number 1 at the base of the clearing kit indicates that the vehicle belongs to the 1st Platoon. At the rear of the hull, above the right-hand track we can see the word "Telephone" with an arrow pointing upwards to indicate the caisson where the telephone for liaising with the infantry was located. (USMC HD)

[15] One of the Shermans was equipped with a bulldozer blade in the HQ Platoon in each company which also included an M32B2 recovery vehicle.

[16] The geometric shapes were not applied on the sides nor on the front of the hull. This enabled this unit to be dissociated from the Tank Company, 22nd Marines, which used identical markings (shapes and sizes), but which painted them on the front and the hull sides during the battle of Guam.

Left: For the Guam campaign, the 3rd Tank Battalion was entirely reequipped with Sherman medium tanks. Here we can see the 2nd Platoon of C Company during a pause. The numbers were painted white on the four sides of the turrets. On some tanks, a yellow triangle pointing downwards was also added on the gun shield (No. 72, 74, and 76) and referred to the Special Troops. The tanks did not have a name in this platoon. (NARA)

Examples of B Company names for the Guam campaign

Tactical Marking	Name
Triangle 1	*Butcher*
Square ?	*Black Widow*
Square 4	*Tokyo Express*
Triangle 2 (dozer)	*The Guy Black* (formerly called *Tarantula*)
Square 5*	*King Kong*
Circle 1	*Dynamite*
Circle 2	*Marauder*
M32B2 (not numbered)	*Battlin*

* On Guam, each company was equipped with 14 tanks shared out into three platoons of four plus the HQ Section. A film taken on Guadalcanal in the spring of 1944 shows the tanks from B Company parading: they were numbered up to 5 indicating that the platoons had numbered up to five tanks temporarily.

As with A Company, the winged five-point star was painted on the roof of the Shermans. Names were also painted on the hull sides, under the elephant, but followed no specific rule. They did not begin with the company letter, as shown in the table above. Finally, the UNIS 633 marking was painted on the rear extremity of the hull sides and the vehicles showed USMC registration numbers.

C Company had the most complex markings; its tanks were christened with names beginning with a D (and not C). As described above, C Company, 3rd Tank Battalion, was made up of personnel and vehicles coming from the former D Company of the 1st Corps Tank Battalion (medium). When they joined their new unit, the Marines decided to keep the "D" when naming their tanks. The names *Dasher* (No. 80), and *Diablo* (No. 68) have been identified.

A triangle pointing downwards (the symbol of the Special Troops) was also applied to several spots on the tank (turret and hull).

As for the two other companies, the registration numbers, the UNIS marking (634), and the five-point star for aerial identification, were applied to the tanks. Finally, two numbers painted in big white characters on the side of the turret, on the

A Company landing on July 21, 1944. All the tanks bore a name beginning with the letter A, except for the tankdozer visible here. A large number was painted on the rear at the base of the fording kit. No. 6 is visible in the background on the left of the photograph. (NARA)

Above: These M4A2s belonging to B Company are leaving their bivouac on the island of Guam. They all come from different platoons as indicated by the geometric shapes painted on the turrets. We can see tanks from the HQ Section (triangle), the 1st and 2nd Platoons (square and circle). (NARA)

Right: Behind this Type 95 from the tank unit of the 29th Japanese division on Guam, we can see the tankdozer of B Company, Triangle 2, christened *The Guy Black*. The name and the tactical insignia on the turret are painted white. (NARA)

M3 AND M4 TANKS OF THE 3RD TANK BATTALION, 1943–1944

M3A1, Diamond 3, 3rd Platoon, C Company, Bougainville, November 1943.

M4A2 (mid-production), No. 5, *Angel*, 2nd Platoon, A Company, Guam, July 1944.

M4A2 (mid-production), Circle 2, *Marauder*, 2nd Platoon, B Company, Guam, July 1944.

Above: *Adamzapple* from A Company still sports the elephant of the 1st Corps Tank Battalion (medium). It was painted yellow, as was the registration number USMC 72881. The name was painted gray. The profile of a Native American woman has been drawn in chalk on the side of the tank next to the name. (NARA)

Below: *Dasher*, No. 80 of C Company, belonged to the 3rd Platoon. The hull side is covered with a number of markings as shown by the color profile on page 76. (NARA via Morgan Gillard)

gun shield, and on the rear side of the hull, enabled the vehicle to be identified in the company.

The first number indicated the platoon and the second, the position of the tank in the platoon. Thus, the series of the 50s indicated the HQ Section, 60, 70, and 80 respectively the 1st, 2nd, and 3rd Platoons.

Numbers and names of A Company on Guam	
Tank number	Associated name
1	*Atabrine*
2	*Angel*
3	?
4	*Ace*
5	*Agony*
6	*Atlas*
7	*Ann*
8	*Apache*
9	*Ateball*
10	?
11	?
12	?
13	*Andrea*
14	*Adder*
15	?
M32B2 (not numbered)	*Almighty*

Above: Two M4A2s from A Company advancing on a road on Guam a short while after landing. The vehicles still carry their homemade fording kits with open 50-gallon drums acting as exhausts. The winged white star on the turret is easily visible. On the hull above each track appear the letters "USMC" painted yellow; on the right, the inscription is hidden by the .30-caliber ammunition box converted into a telephone liaison box. (NARA)

Below: Despite what common sense would have us believe, the 3rd Tank Battalion had no D Company in 1944. Indeed, the tanks from C Company on Guam all bore names beginning with the letter D, such as *Dagwood*. This was due to the transfer of personnel and vehicles of the former D Company, 1st Corps Tank Battalion (medium) at the time the 3rd Tank Battalion was being totally reorganized at the beginning of 1944. (NARA via Morgan Gillard)

Below: Rear view of the platoon leader's tank of 2nd Platoon, B Company. The style and the size of the tactical markings used by this unit were very similar to those used by the Tank Company, 22nd Marines, which was fighting on Guam at the same time. However, several details enable us to differentiate them, especially the elephant and the name painted on the sides of the tanks in B Company. The latter also bore the UNIS marking on the flanks towards the rear: a flattened diamond with the number 633 painted yellow on the inside. (NARA)

Above left: A color photograph taken from a 1944 film showing the markings on the hull and the turret of Circle 1 *Dynamite*, the tank of the 2nd Platoon's leader from B Company. Note the USMC registration number 76762 and the unit's mascot painted yellow. (USMC HD and USC)

Above right: Circle 2 of 2nd Platoon, B Company, had all the typical markings of this unit. Although barely visible on this photo, the name *Marauder* has been painted under the elephant. (NARA)

Right: In the spring of 1944, experiments were carried out using M4A2s from C Company, 3rd Tank Battalion, to equip them with rocket launchers. This project came to nothing. This unit's markings were rather visible: we can see the five-point stars at the rear of the turret, the UNIS markings (yellow) and the triangle (yellow) pointing downwards above the right-hand track. (NARA)

Iwo Jima (February–March 1945)

As indicated above, the M4A2s used by the 3rd Tank Battalion on Guam were redeployed on Iwo Jima except for the destroyed tanks that were replaced by late model M4A2s before the new campaign.

The battalion was reorganized with three companies of 15 tanks each, including a recovery vehicle. The battalion commander also had a command Sherman.[17]

As a result, the markings used by the three companies were very similar to those used on Guam. They were nonetheless adapted to the new company organization, with five three-tank platoons. Furthermore, armor plating was welded onto the sides of the hull, hiding the original names and the elephant, the unit's mascot.

As it did on Guam, A Company numbered its tanks from 1–15. The 1st, 2nd, 3rd, and 4th Platoons were respectively identified by the numbers 1–3, 4–6, 7–9, and 10–12. The HQ Platoon had tanks No. 13, 14, and 15, the last one being fitted with a bulldozer blade. An M32B2 was also available in the maintenance section, attached to the HQ Platoon. The numbers were painted yellow on the lower part of the fording kit as well as on the sides of the turret, so as to make identification easier.

A Company put the names of its tanks on the recently welded armor plating. However, the association number–name seemed to differ from Guam, as revealed by the tank *Angel* which bears the identification No. 2 as compared with No. 5 on Guam. Within B Company, the symbols designating the 1st, 2nd, and 3rd Platoons were maintained. The triangle now designated the 4th, whereas the tanks in HQ Platoon were not given a shape and were simply numbered 1, 2, and 3 on the turret.

Names were painted on the hull's additional armor plates but only a few of them were identified. The only known examples were *Caribou*, *Nip Clipper* (No. 2, HQ Platoon), and *The Guy Black* (No. 3, tankdozer).

C Company numbers and nicknames, Iwo Jima

HQ Platoon	1st Platoon	2nd Platoon	3rd Platoon	4th Platoon
52 *Dagwood*	62 *Dimple*	72 (no name, formerly *Doodle-bug*)	82	92
54 (no name) (tankdozer, formerly *Destroyer*)*	64 (no name)	74	84	94
56	66 *Demagog*	76 *Dood-It*	86	96 *Demigod*
Dude (M32B2, no number)	-	-	-	-

* Some sources indicated that the tank bore the name *Dozer* at Iwo Jima, but the photographs do not show any names painted on the hull sides. A name—perhaps *Dozer*—appears on the tank's cannon. *Destry II* and *Domdor* also existed but the names cannot be associated to a number because of a lack of pictures.

17 The battalion commander already had a command Sherman on Guam, though this was not regulation.

The 3rd Battalion kept its old M4A2s for the battle of Iwo Jima. A few modifications were undertaken to improve protection of the vehicles and the crews; 2-inch steel plates were added to the flanks of the hull to where ammunition was stored, and on the right-hand side of the turret—the tank's less-armored point. Here is tank No. 66 of the 1st Platoon, C Company, on Iwo Jima. The name of the tank, as well as the elephant, has been covered by the welded armor plates. (NARA)

M4 TANKS OF THE 3RD TANK BATTALION, 1944

M4A2 (mid-production), No. 78,
2nd Platoon, C Company, Guam, July 1944.

M4A2 (mid-production), No. 14, *Adder*, HQ Platoon, A Company, Iwo Jima, February 1945.

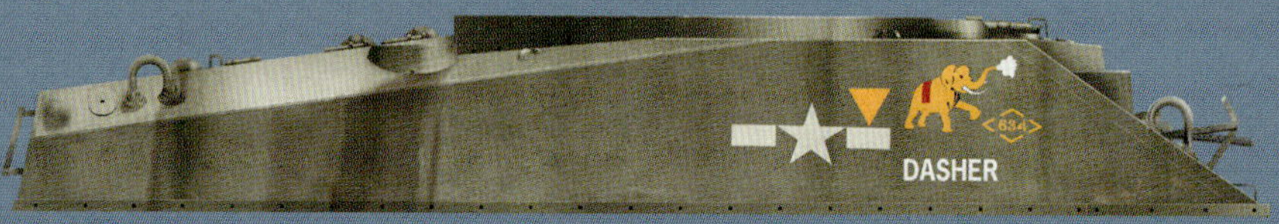

M4A2 (mid-production), No. 80, *Dasher*,
3rd Platoon, C Company, Guam, July 1944.

Above: This view of the 3rd Tank Battalion command post on Motoyama airfield enables us to appreciate how relevant the colors chosen for the tank markings were. On the right, A Company and its yellow turret markings (tank number) are barely visible at this distance. On the other hand, on the left, the white markings on C Company's tanks are clearer. (NARA)

Right: This photograph enables us to appreciate the markings used by A Company on Iwo Jima. They were yellow except for the winged star at the rear of the turret which was white. We can see the UNIS markings at the bottom on the left of the photo. (NARA via Scott Freund)

Below right: A photograph of the tank *Atabrine* No. 1 on Iwo Jima. The tank's number is painted yellow on the turret. The USMC registration number 72803 in the center of the picture indicates that this is one of the battalion's original vehicles. (NARA via Scott Freund)

Left: *Double Trouble* was B Company's command tank. Following the new organization of the tank units at the end of 1944, the HQ Platoon abandoned using the triangle for identifying its vehicles. The shape now indicates the 4th Platoon. The HQ Platoon numbered its tanks from 1–3 but did not have a geometric shape on Iwo. According to Robert Reibe—one of the crew members—the tank's name referred to the "trouble for our repair shop and trouble for those Japs." The registration number 100534 reveals here a new replacement vehicle obtained after the battle of Guam. The other markings are 4-G-4644 and SCR508 (the model of radio equipping the tank). (USMC HD)

Right: *Destroyer* was a vehicle from C Company's stocks, converted into a tankdozer before the landing on Iwo Jima and rechristened *Dozer* by its crew. It can be seen here on Guam before the 1945 battle. Except for the number on the turret, all the other markings visible on this photo were covered by the modifications to come. (NARA)

Above: *Almighty*, the recovery vehicle from A Company, still bears the 1st Corps Tank Battalion (medium) marking on its flanks when it was deployed on Iwo Jima in 1945. This image enables us to see the other markings of the M32B2—the USMC 85549 number and the name *Lulla* painted on the driver's post. (NARA)

Left: After Guam, A Company painted the number of its tanks in yellow on the turret to make identification easier by the other vehicles. The tank called *Apache* bears the number 8 and is seen here in full action on Iwo Jima on February 25, 1945. (NARA)

Above left: *Nip Clipper*, an M4A2 from B Company destroyed at Iwo Jima. One can guess at the markings on the turret partly rubbed off: a diamond with the number 1 inside it. Originally, the vehicle belonged to the 4th Platoon (Triangle Platoon), but its turret was replaced by one from another tank during the fighting. (NARA via Estes)

Above right: *Aileen*, No. 77, was the battalion commander's tank, seen here embarking for the operations on Iwo Jima. It bore the registration number USMC 100692. Note the black, greased canvas around the turret and the gun shield to make the vehicle watertight. (USMC HD and USC)

Below: This picture of an M4A2 from C Company landing on Iwo Jima on February 23, 1945, shows the turret marking for the aerial observers. It was applied before the landings on Guam, and the 3rd Tank Battalion kept it for Iwo Jima. (NARA via Morgan Gillard)

M4 TANKS OF THE 3RD TANK BATTALION, 1945

M4A2 (mid-production), Triangle 2, *Nip Clipper*, 4th Platoon, B Company, Iwo Jima, February 1945.

M4A2 (mid-production), No. 96, *Demigod*, 4th Platoon, C Company, Iwo Jima, February 1945.

6 The Tank Company, 4th Marines

As indicated in the previous chapter, the Tank Company, 4th Marines was the new name for the former A Company, 3rd Tank Battalion, after this unit had taken part in the landings on Emirau.

The unit also received 18 new M4A2s. In May 1944, the 4th Marines was associated to another regiment, the 22nd Marines, to form the 1st Provisional Marine Brigade. The company only took part in the fighting on Guam in the summer of 1944 as the Tank Company, 4th Marines.

Indeed, the addition of a third regiment (29th Marines) in the fall of 1944 enabled a new division—the 6th Marine Division—to be formed.

The Tank Company, 4th Marines then became A Company, 6th Tank Battalion in October 1944 (see Chapter 10).

Guam (July–August 1944)

The tactical markings were inherited directly from A Company, 3rd Tank Battalion.

The platoons were identified by large geometrical shapes applied by stencil on the center of the glacis, on the fording kit, and the turret. As with many other tank companies of the period, the 1st, 2nd, and 3rd Platoons were identified respectively by a square, a circle, and a diamond; and the HQ Platoon by a cloverleaf.

A Company, 3rd Tank Battalion, was detached to the 4th Marines for the assault on Emirau. This association lasted and the unit became the Tank Company, 4th Marines. It kept the markings with big geometric shapes as can be seen on these M4A2s on Guam. The circle indicates the 2nd Platoon. (NARA)

Above: Square 5 from the 1st Platoon on Guam. The markings of the Tank Company, 4th Marines, were much bigger than those used by the 3rd Tank Battalion or the Tank Company, 22nd Marines. Moreover, they were painted yellow, whereas the other two units used white paint. (NARA)

Right: As well as the tactical markings identifying the vehicle, the unit imagined a symbol which was unique in the USMC. All the tanks had a gray rhinoceros charging in the dust on their flanks. The elephant and the rhinoceros were symbols currently used by the armored units in all countries. (Bob Botts via Ed Gilbert)

Below: As well as the rhinoceros and the tactical markings, the company's tanks all had their registration number on the rear part of the hull sides. In the center, the letters "TC" were also painted white, but their meaning remains unknown. (NARA)

There was a number inside the geometric shape from 1–5 (1–3 in the case of the HQ Platoon) indicating the tank's position in the platoon.

The USMC format of the registration number was painted on the rear part of the flanks of the hull while in the center, the letters "TC"—whose meaning remains unknown—appeared in small letters.

Finally, the company chose a rhinoceros charging in the dust as its mascot. Painted by hand on the hull sides, it was quickly covered over by additional armor plating. The crews were, however, attached to their insignia and hastened to draw the rhino on this plating.

Top: The M4A2 with the registration number USMC 79656 belonged to the 2nd Platoon. Note the imposing size of the turret markings. (NARA)

Above: The cloverleaf indicated the HQ Platoon. The tankdozer of the Tank Company was the only tank in the unit to have been christened by its crew. (NARA)

Left: A color photo from a 1944 film showing Clover 1 of HQ Platoon, landing on Guam on July 21. The tactical markings (shape and number) were painted yellow. (NARA)

Although not attested, a five-point star was probably painted on the roof of the tanks, as was the habit for operations in the Marianas.

M4A2 (mid-production), Diamond 2, 3rd Platoon, Tank Company, 4th Marines, 1st Provisional Marine Brigade, Guam, July 1944.

Diamond 4, 3rd Platoon, supporting a group of Marines on Guam, summer of 1944. The ammunition box bolted to the rear above the right-hand track housed the tank–infantry liaison telephone. (USMC HD)

7 The 2nd Separate Tank Company/Tank Company, 22nd Marines

The origins of this unit go back to 1942 when the Marine Corps decided to activate two independent tank companies (Separate Tank Companies).

They were supposed to receive the Marmon-Herrington tankettes that nobody wanted because they had only mediocre performance. Assigned respectively to the 3rd Marines and 22nd Marines, the 1st and 2nd Separate Tank Companies were deployed in the Pacific in a purely defensive role.

After several months spent in the Samoan Islands, they were reequipped with M3A1 light tanks. The 1st Separate Tank Company was absorbed into the 3rd Tank Battalion, while the 2nd Separate Tank Company remained active: it was reequipped with 15 M4A2 Sherman tanks[18] and took part in the fighting on Eniwetok Atoll in February 1944. In May 1944, it was renamed Tank Company, 22nd Marines, obtained 17 new M4A2s[19] (including one tankdozer) and was incorporated into the 1st Provisional Marine Brigade. It took part in the battle of Guam in the summer of 1944. It subsequently became B Company of the 6th Tank Battalion when the 6th Marine Division was created (see Chapter 10).

Eniwetok (February 1944)

The 2nd Separate Tank Company adopted the traditional system of geometric shapes to identify its platoons.

The 1st, 2nd, and 3rd Platoons were identified by a square, a circle, and a diamond. The HQ Platoon was identified by a triangle. As with the other units, a number (from 1–4, or 1–3 for the HQ Platoon) was painted within the geometric shape to indicate the tank's position in the platoon.

This tactical marking was painted on the sides and rear of the turret, on the glacis, the sides, and rear of the hull. A name was put on the turret on one or both sides in front of the geometric shape. The name had to start with the platoon letter, an S for the 1st (Square) Platoon, a C for the 2nd (Circle) Platoon, a D for the 3rd (Diamond) Platoon, and finally, a T for the HQ (Triangle) Platoon.

Tank names and codes for Eniwetok

Tank's name	Associated Code
Caesar	*Circle 1*
Cobra	*Circle 2*
Caboose	*Circle 4*
Shirley	*Square 1*
Dodo	*Diamond No. ?*

The commander of the landing force made the following recommendation after the battle of Eniwetok: "Medium and light tanks are camouflaged to hinder effective recognition. This is all right for their front and sides, but in order to help our air observers and air attack groups, all tank tops should be rendered clearly visible from the air. Recommendation: that tops of medium and light tanks be painted with prominent and readily distinguishable markings."

There were two events which explained this decision (see page 91).

18 Six of these tanks came from the former C Company, 1st Corps Tank Battalion (medium), having fought at Tarawa.

19 The company's structure was identical at Eniwerok, i.e. three platoons of four tanks, plus the HQ Platoon with three tanks. This time the company benefitted from having two replacement tanks.

Above: The 1st and 2nd Separate Tank Companies were set up with the USMC's Marmon-Herrington tankettes. Here, the 1st Separate Tank Company has been photographed in the Samoan Islands in September 1942. This mixed unit was made up of several models: CTL6 in the center, CTM3TBD on the right, and M3 at the rear. The unit was renamed C Company, 3rd Tank Battalion in March 1943. Note the markings made up of geometric shapes and numbers to indicate the platoons and vehicles. (NARA via Ken Estes)

Left: The M3A1s of the 2nd Separate Tank Company did not have any tactical markings. These appeared on the Shermans which were received a short while before the fighting on Eniwetok. Photograph taken in the Samoan Islands in 1943. (NARA via Ken Estes)

Above: A photograph of Triangle 1, the tank of the company commander, Captain Harry Calcutt, on Eniwetok. The tactical markings were painted white. A handful of tanks from this unit had wooden planks on the sides as protection against the magnetic mines. (NARA)

Below left: A photograph taken from a color film shot in Eniwetok Atoll at the beginning of 1944. This is *Shirley* of Square Platoon (1st). Note the sand-colored camouflage applied above the factory olive drab. (NARA)

Below right: *Caboose* was the fourth vehicle of the 2nd Platoon of the 2nd Separate Tank Company. It is interesting to note that the crew has used two colors to paint the name. The letters "CABO" are painted in white and the letters "OSE" are in olive drab. The registration number is hidden by the vegetation. (USMC HD)

Left: Circle 2 *Cobra* from 2nd Platoon shows the two-tone camouflage that was typical of the unit in the Marshall Islands. A canvas sheet has been tightened over the flanks as protection against magnetic mines. On the engine compartment, we can see the mesh wire (partly lifted up and torn off) which had been fixed on for the same reason. (NARA)

Below: Detail of the markings of M4A2 *Shirley* from 1st Platoon. We can see the registration number in the center as well as the USMC emblem, applied with a stencil on the side armor. These elements were painted yellow. Next to the emblem, the black factory markings are still visible. We can also guess at the name *Shirley* painted white on the upper part of the turret and the crew has even christened the barrel *Jane*. (NARA)

Above: The burnt-out wreck of Square 4 lying on Eniwetok Island after suffering an internal explosion. The tactical marking of the tank is visible on the stern, near the jerrycan support. (Naval History and Heritage Command Photo #S487F3.02)

Right: Circle 1 *Caesar* was the 2nd Platoon leader's tank. This photo enables us to appreciate the unique shape of the fording kits designed by this unit. What also made the 2nd Separate Tank Company a precursor was the presence of a microphone at the rear of the tanks so the infantry could communicate its instructions to the crews (not visible here). Eniwetok was the first operation in which this communication system was set up and used by the Marine Corps. (NARA)

Firstly, during the battle, it was extremely difficult for aerial observers to find the frontline because of the rapid progress of the troops on the ground. These were supposed to mark their progression with colored panels, theoretically visible from the sky. The advance was too rapid for these markers to be arranged.

Secondly, on Parry, one of the islands of the Eniwetok Atoll, a naval bombardment was requested by mistake, in a sector where American tanks and infantrymen were moving up; the result was disastrous.

It seems that this recommendation had caught on in the Marine Corps' bureaucratic echelons. Indeed, all the USMC tanks used an aerial identification system during the Mariana campaign in the summer of 1944.

Though the system had been used in different forms (stars, stripes, numbers) and colors (yellow, orange, white), this was the first standardizing directive, common to all units, applicable to all USMC tanks (see appendix 2, page 149).

Guam (July–August 1944)

Renamed Tank Company, 22nd Marines, the unit kept the same codes for marking its tanks. The geometric shapes were painted white on the sides and the rear of the turret, on the front and the rear of the hull, as well as on the base of the fording kit.

On the sides, the symbol was painted towards the engine compartment that enabled Tank Company, 22nd Marines to be differentiated from

Another wreck, that of Diamond 4, photographed on the island of Parry in the Eniwetok Atoll. A 16-inch shell fired from an American battleship destroyed the tank. This mistake led to the tank units adopting visuals painted on the roof of the turrets. The shell probably ricocheted on the ground before hitting the tank. (Naval History and Heritage Command Photo #S487F3.02)

Above left: Two M4A2s from the Tank Company, 22nd Marines recently disembarked on Guam on July 21, 1944. The unit used several types of fording kits. The rear base is the one the unit designed for the Eniwetok campaign, on which a standard factory-designed exhaust has been mounted. The air intake for the engine (not seen here) was a 50-gallon drum. (NARA)

Above right: Photo taken from a color film showing Square 2 *Scrappy* from 1st Platoon. The tactical markings are visible on the turret and on the glacis of the M4A2. (NARA)

B Company of the 3rd Tank Battalion that used a marking system which was very similar in style and dimensions on Guam.

The name is applied again in front, on the geometric shapes painted on the sides of the tanks' turrets, and followed the same rules as for Eniwetok: the name began with the platoon's call sign.

The names *El Toro* (Triangle 1), *Dood-it* (Diamond 4), *Scrappy* (Square 2), *Satan* (Square 1), *Cobra 2* (Circle 3), and *Tokyo Rose* (Triangle 3) were used on Guam.

Two types of new markings were applied for the battle of Guam. Big winged five-point stars were painted on the roof of each tank for aerial identification. On several vehicles, graduations of 0–360 degrees were painted on the base of the turret and probably allowed the platoon leaders to adjust the azimuth of the other tanks.

Right: This photo of the 1st Platoon command tank, Square 1 *Satan*, shows the markings of the turret and in particular, the graduations on the base. The zero was painted near the base of the commander's hatch (rear right). The use of these graduations is not mentioned in official reports. The winged star for aerial identification is also visible on the top of the turret. (NARA)

M4 TANKS OF THE 2ND SEPARATE TANK COMPANY AND OF THE TANK COMPANY, 22ND MARINES, 1944

M4A2 (mid-production), Circle 1, *Caesar*, 2nd Platoon, 2nd Separate Tank Company, Eniwetok, February 1944.

M4A2 (mid-production), Triangle 3, *Tokyo Rose*, HQ Platoon, Tank Company, 22nd Marines, 1st Provisional Marine Brigade, Guam, July 1944.

Left: The M32B2 recovery vehicle of the Tank Company, 22nd Marines, was called *Nut Butter*. This vehicle was the only one to keep the sand camouflage used on Eniwetok. The other tanks were either olive drab, or camouflaged with a lighter tone of olive drab. (Bob Botts via Ed Gilbert)

Below: The tank of the company commander, Triangle 1 *El Toro*, on Guam. The turret markings were painted white. The geometric shape and the tank number were also painted on the rear part of the hull sides which enabled this unit to be distinguished from B Company, 3rd Tank Battalion, which used markings of a similar size and color. Guam was the last time this unit used wooden planks because Japanese shells were able to break this additional armor, as can be seen on this image. (NARA)

Above: Another color photo, this time of Circle 3 *Cobra 2* from 2nd Platoon. Note the pale green applied as camouflage over the factory-painted olive drab. (NARA)

Right: M4A2 *Dood-it* of 3rd Platoon on Guam. This tank bears the turret graduations that were not in general use in the unit. (USMC HD)

Below: Another photo coming from the 1944 color film showing Triangle 3 *Tokyo Rose* on Guam. The triangle and the number were painted white, whereas the name of the tank is yellow. Note the camouflage made up of two different shades of olive drab. (NARA)

8 The 4th Tank Battalion

The 4th Tank Battalion was officially created on May 12, 1943, and as with the 3rd Tank Battalion, its companies were activated on the East and West Coasts of the United States. Thc 4th Tank Battalion and the remainder of the 4th Marine Division left the continent at the beginning of 1944 to take part directly in the Marshall Islands campaign.

The mixed battalion was thus composed of two companies of light tanks and one company of M4A2 medium tanks and was attached to the division's Special Troops.

The battalion took part in the fighting on the various islets making up the Kwajalein Atoll between January 31 and February 4, 1944. It was reorganized the following spring in Hawaii: its three companies were now equipped with M4A2 Shermans. A fourth company was activated with Stuart M3A1 Satan flamethrowers and a few M5A1s.

From June to August 1944, the 4th Tank Battalion took part in the Mariana campaign (Saipan and Tinian).

In the fall, the battalion was once again reorganized; detached from the divisional HQ, it functioned semi-autonomously.

Entirely reequipped with Sherman M4A3s, it took part in its last campaign in February and March 1945 on Iwo Jima. It returned to the United States in October 1945 where it was disbanded.

Front view of the command M5A1 of B Company, 4th Tank Battalion, *Hunter*, in its LCM, on the way to the island of Namur in the Kwajalein Atoll. Note the cream-colored stripe on the glacis. (USMC HD)

Kwajalein Atoll (January–February 1944)

The 4th Tank Battalion companies were all equipped with 18 vehicles, shared out into three platoons of five tanks each plus an HQ Platoon with three tanks. A and B Companies were equipped with M5A1 Stuarts. The HQ Platoon also had an M32B2.

C Company was easy to identify since this was the only unit to be equipped with M4A2s at Roi-Namur (Kwajalein Atoll).

To identify its vehicles, the battalion used markings that were rather elaborate, starting with the UNIS markings. Painted yellow, they were categorized by the half-moon of the 4th Marine Division and the numbers 131, 132, 133, or 134 painted inside them. The first number (1) indicated the divisional HQ to which the tanks were attached; the second (3) indicated the tank

Above: Another view aboard the LCM transporting Lieutenant Denig's tank in the Marshall Islands showing the white five-point star on the gunner's hatch on the left. (USMC HD)

Left: *Hothead* was another M5A1 from HQ Platoon of A Company. In front of the tank's name is the UNIS marking with the half-moon of the 4th Marine Division. Inside it, the code 133 indicated the divisional HQ (1) to which the tanks (3) were attached at the beginning of the war. The last number indicated B Company (3). (NARA)

Above: The M5A1 *Gallion* from 3rd Platoon, B Company, shown bogged down on the beach at Namur. The shape of the camouflage stripes is very varied in this unit. We can make out the UNIS marking placed before the name of the tank. (NARA)

Right: This photo taken on Namur after the fighting shows an M32B2 and some M4A2s from C Company. The first letter of the name reflected its platoon and its company. The L was attributed to the HQ Platoon. The other vehicles visible are *Killer* (3rd Platoon), *Jungle Jim* (2nd Platoon, top right), and *Juarez* (2nd Platoon, top left). (USMC HD)

Below: The M4A2 *King Kong* was the tank of Lieutenant Gearl M. English, the commander of the 3rd Platoon, C Company. The name has been painted in big white letters on the flanks, fitted with wooden planks to prevent magnetic mines from sticking. The glacis has been covered with plywood for the same reason. Note the camouflage of the turret consisting of sand-colored splotches. (NARA)

battalion and the last number was the company: 1 for the H&S Company, 2 for A Company, and so on. Note however that C Company did not use the UNIS markings on its M4A2s.

Names completed the companies' identification according to a sequential system. Thus the name of the tanks in A Company started with the letters A, B, C, and D and designated respectively the 1st, 2nd, and 3rd Platoons and the HQ Platoon. B Company was given the letters E, F, G, and H, and C Company the letters I, J, K, and L.

Few photographs showed the tanks from A and B Companies on Kwajalein. *Deacon* is the only known example from A Company (HQ Platoon). *Hothead*, *Hunter*, *Hornet*, *Express*, *Fury*, *Flame*, *Force*, and *Gallion* are known to have been in B Company.

C Company is comparatively better documented in terms of photographs. The list of names is in the table on page 101.

Below left: Photos of another vehicle from C Company on which the crew has applied a camouflage scheme consisting of blotches of sand-colored paint, this time on the turret and the rear fording kit.

Below right: This is the M4A2 *Inquisitive* from the 1st Platoon. (USMC HD)

Above: This photo was taken on Roi-Namur and shows tanks from 2nd Platoon, C Company. As can be seen, the name of the tank was not painted on the rear fording kit and the unit did not have infantry-tank liaison telephones. The Stuart fuel tank containing water has not yet been installed, either. (USMC HD)

Right: *Jungle Jim* was the name of a famous cartoon character of the 1940s. The M4A2 was commanded by the youngest tank commander in the unit, Sergeant Jerry Ingram, aged 17 at the time. The 2nd Platoon, C Company, was the only one to use a tank number made up of two numbers. The first indicated the platoon, the second the position of the vehicle within the platoon. Note that the photo has been taken at the same spot as that showing *King Kong* (see page 98). (NARA)

The Marianas (June–August 1944)

The marking system used by the 4th Tank Battalion remained unchanged for Saipan, and Tinian.

A and B Companies were reequipped with M4A2s,[20] with 14 tanks each, of which one was a tankdozer. The arrangement of three platoons of four tanks, plus the HQ Section with two tanks, was in use at the time. An M32B2 was in the HQ Platoon for maintenance.

C Company used 18 new M4A2s instead of the 14 authorized and kept the structure it used during the preceding campaign.

The 13 Stuart light tanks converted into flamethrowers were regrouped in D Company which was given the UNIS 135 marking with the letters M, N, O, and P to designate its tanks.

In reality, the letter O was not used and the tanks received numbers instead. Five M5A1s were used to make up the numbers in D Company and were used for command and close-quarters protection for the Satans.

The medium tank companies painted the names on the hull sides and occasionally in the middle of the glacis. The size of the names was relatively modest in the case of A Company; this was a source of confusion during the fighting. Names were painted on the turret sides in the case of the light tanks.

The names were painted yellow in the case of the M5A1s and white for the M4A2s. The crews of the latter occasionally painted a slogan or a name on the tank's gun barrel.

Tank Names, Saipan, summer of 1944

	HQ Platoon/section	1st Platoon	2nd Platoon	3rd Platoon
A Company	*Ding-Dong* ? ? (M32B2)	*Apache* (tankdozer) *Ann* *Ace* ?	*Bacchus* ? ? ?	*Corsair* *Cavalier* ? ?
B Company	*Hothead III* ? ? (M32B2)	[a] [a] [a] [a]	*Fireball* *Flivver* ? ?	*Goldbrick* *Goony Boid III* *Geronimo* *Gremlin IV*
C Company	*Ill Wind*[b] *Impatient Virgin* *Lulubelle* (M32B2)	*Invincible* *Invader* *Ironsides* *Inquisitive* *Illustrious*	*Jungle Jim II* *Juarez* *Joker* (tankdozer) *Jenny Lee* *Jeezbel*	*King Kong* *Killer* *Knave 3rd* *Kapu* *Kickapoo*
D Company	*Pancho* *Pappy* *The Profiteer*[c] - -	*Margaret*[c] *Miami Special*[c] *Mufsaid* ? ?	*Nannie*[c] *Nobby* ? ? ?	54[c] 55 58 ? ?

a. The tanks from the 1st Platoon of B Company apparently had no names.

b. *Ill Wind* was the command tank of C Company. It should have had a name starting with the letter L, but for some unknown reason, the crew selected a name beginning with the letter I. This was the same for the tank *Impatient Virgin*.

c. M5A1.

[20] B Company received several reconditioned vehicles to reach the standard allocation of 14 tanks.

On Saipan on June 16, 1944, the D Company tanks' mission was to join C Company with a view to destroying resistance points. D Company had a lot of trouble trying to find C Company because of the poor visibility of the tank names: "Company 'A' was operating in an area nearby and was mistaken for Company 'C' until we were near enough to see the names of their tanks."

It is interesting to note that C Company kept the names it used during the Marshall Islands campaign, whereas B Company used new ones. Names were often painted on the barrels of the Shermans in C Company. The gunner in *Ill Wind* chose *Heaven Can Wait*, *King Kong* chose *Exterminator*, and *Destroyer* was painted on *Inquisitive*'s barrel. The name was painted yellow on one side only of the barrel.

After Saipan had been secured, B Company was reequipped with 14 new M4A2 tanks and the 3rd Platoon entirely renamed its vehicles: *Goldbrick Jr.*, *Gung Ho II*, *Gizmo*, and *Goony Boid IV*.

As a general rule, the names were painted white in the four companies.

The flamethrower tanks from D Company were often assigned to a company of medium tanks that protected them during assaults against fortified enemy positions.

Following the recommendation made after the Marshall Islands about identifying the tanks from the air (see Chapter 7), the report on 4th Marine Division's operations on Saipan indicated that "Our tanks were also painted with a yellow panel on the top side which facilitated easy identification from the air."

Within B Company, the tank number (within the battalion) was painted red over the yellow paint. However, this big yellow marking had a disadvantage in that it made the tanks more visible to the enemy who were set up on the heights.

Above: *Illustrious* was another M4A2 belonging to 1st Platoon, C Company. We can see the first letters of the name, *Widow Maker*, painted on the right-hand side of the barrel. It was reused on *Comet* on Iwo Jima. (USMC HD)

Below: Originally, the half-tracks armed with a 75 mm cannon were intended as tank destroyers. However, during the Pacific War they played a more defensive role on the airfields or in direct support of the infantry for reducing pillboxes and bunkers. In the background, we can see several M4A2s from C Company regrouped on Roi-Namur. (Naval History and Heritage Command Photo #5487F19.01)

M5 AND M4 TANKS OF THE 4TH MARINE TANK BATTALION, 1944

M5A1, *The Deacon*, HQ Platoon, A Company, Kwajalein Atoll, January 1944.

M5A1, *Fury*, 2nd Battalion, B Company, Kwajalein Atoll, February 1944.

M4A2 (mid-production), No. 24, *Jezebel*, 2nd Platoon, C Company, Kwajalein Atoll, February 1944.

Top: A photo of *King Kong* from 3rd Platoon, C Company, taken on Saipan. The name has been painted white on the rear part of the fording kit. On the left, between the kit and the box for the field telephone, the "Target Clock" has been painted in black for infantry to guide the tank's fire. The sand-colored camouflage is still being used on the turret and the roof has been painted yellow for aerial identification. The inscription *Exterminator* is barely visible on the gun barrel. (NARA)

Middle: The M4A2 *Ace* from 1st Platoon, A Company, supporting the advancing infantry on Tinian. Camouflage imitating the vegetation has been applied after the battle of Saipan. The tank's name has been painted white. (NARA)

Below: A photo taken from a 1944 film showing the tank *Bacchus* from 2nd Platoon, A Company, 4th Tank Battalion. Note the sand-colored camouflage on the M4A2. (NARA)

Above: *Knave 3rd*, another M4A2 from 3rd Platoon, C Company, has been temporarily immobilized on Saipan after having rolled over a mine. We can see the camouflage made of long undulating lines on the turret and the vehicle's sides. C Company was the only one to use wood as anti-magnetic mine protection during the Mariana Islands campaign. (NARA)

Left: *Ding Dong* was put out of action on the second day of the battle of Saipan by 75 mm gunfire. It belonged to the HQ Section of A Company. Note the name's small size, making it particularly difficult to read at a distance. (NARA)

Right: A photo taken during the last days of the battle for Saipan, at Marpi Point, to the north of the island, showing a combination of tanks from various companies operating together on the aerodrome. Note the checkerboard camouflage on the two Shermans on the right. Although similar, they belong to two different companies: the one on the right to B Company (it had no name), the one in the center (called *Bacchus*) belonged to A Company. The M5A1 was from D Company. (NARA)

Below: Another photograph taken on June 15, 1944, of M4A2 *Bacchus* from A Company. This image enables us to appreciate the checkerboard camouflage scheme consisting of yellow sand and pale olive drab painted over the factory-applied olive drab. Below the name, we can see the symbol associated with the Greek divinity: a bunch of grapes in a bowl. (NARA)

Below: The 37 mm cannon of the M5A1s in D Company did not make them very useful for destroying strongpoints. They were mainly used for protecting the flamethrowers. Here we can see *Miami Special* from 1st Platoon. (NARA)

An M4A2 called *Fireball* is loaded aboard an LCM off Saipan, June 15, 1944. It belongs to the 2nd Platoon. We can see the roof of the turret painted yellow, on which the tank's number (23) has been painted red. This practice was unique to B Company. (NARA via Morgan Gillard)

Above: D Company painted the name of its tanks on the side of the turrets like here, *Nobby* from 2nd Platoon. This is one of the 13 M3A1s in the battalion converted into flamethrowers for operating in the Marianas. (NARA)

Right: The tankdozer from A Company, *Apache*, bore the profile of a Native American warrior. Note the UNIS 132 marking in the center of the hull side. The half-moon, the emblem of the 4th Marine Division, is not visible. (NARA)

Above and below: Photos of the tank *Knave 3rd* taken at Hawaii after the fighting in the Marianas. We can see the markings which were covered beforehand by the additional armor made up of oak planks. We can also see *Jungle Jim II* in the background on one of the photos. The periscope of the tank commanders in C Company was surmounted by a little armored cupola to protect it from the firing. The periscope was indeed slightly heightened compared with the original configuration, enabling better visibility within the close quarters of the tank. Note the Japanese 47 mm shell impacts which have pierced the armor but not destroyed the tank on Tinian. (Collection of Sergeant Major Bert R. Nave)

Above: Towards the end of June, several tanks were covered with a thick layer of dust because they were moving around on terrain consisting of white clay (kaolinite). On the tank commander's hatch still open on the closest vehicle, we can see part of the number painted red on a yellow background, meaning this was a vehicle from B Company. (NARA)

Left middle and below: Sergeant Parker's M4A2, *Jenny Lee* from the 2nd Platoon of C Company. The name was imposed by the tank commander, without the latter revealing the name's origin. The Stuart's fuel tank containing water for the infantry has made its appearance on the Shermans of C Company. (NARA)

Left and below: *Corsair* was an M4A2 from the 3rd Platoon, A Company. The designation system used by the tank battalion for its tanks was complex but well-thought-out. Sequences of four initials were attributed to each company and each letter was associated to a platoon within the company. A Company benefitted from the initials A, B, C, and D to name its tanks. On both photos, the vehicles are nonetheless different. The first shows *Corsair* on Saipan before the Japanese destroyed it on July 4, 1944. The second illustrates the replacement tank received in time for the battle of Tinian. (NARA)

A photograph of *Goldbrick Jr.* from 3rd Platoon, B Company, on Tinian. This company was reequipped with a number of late production M4A2s after Saipan. The tank bears the registration number 100541 stenciled yellow. The name and the UNIS markings were painted white. (NARA via Ed Gilbert)

Gizmo is another replacement tank acquired by B Company after Saipan. It bears the USMC number 100545. (NARA)

Above: *Ill Wind* was the tank of C Company's commander. It should have been christened with a name beginning with an L, but for some unexplained reason, the crew chose a name beginning with an I. We note that plywood covers the glacis, and the sides have planks to protect the tank from magnetic mines. (NARA via Ed Gilbert)

Left: A partial side view of *Goony Boid IV* from 3rd Platoon, B Company, on Tinian. The name was painted white. (NARA)

Above: The M5A1, *Margaret*, from 1st Platoon, D Company, on Saipan. The name was painted white and the UNIS marking yellow. (NARA via ED Gilbert)

Right: No. 58 was an M3A1 Satan from 3rd Platoon, D Company. Note the whitened aspect of the tank. (NARA)

Iwo Jima (February–March 1945)

During the fall of 1944, the 4th Tank Battalion started to use the new organization of the USMC's tank units. As a result, the tanks were detached from Division H&S and became an autonomous unit. This was reflected in the adoption of new UNIS markings, now with the numbers 911, 912, 913, and 914 to designate H&S, A, B, and C companies, where the number 9 identifies the tank battalion. The three line companies also abandoned the complex system of nomenclature associated with the platoon and used a more classic system, where the tank's name began with the company's letter: A, B, or C. The name, painted yellow in large characters, was associated with a number indicating the position of the tank in the battalion. A sequence of numbers was attributed to each company, with 1–16 for A Company; 17–32 for B Company; and 33–51 for C Company. H&S Company had two tanks, and the names began with D.

Except for B Company, the numbers were painted on the tank's hull, next to the name. B Company painted the number on the tank track links welded to the sides of the turret.

The crews also painted inscriptions on the gun barrel from time to time. A short while before landing on Iwo Jima, the 4th Tank Battalion received four M4A3 75 (W)s whose cannon had been modified as a flamethrower. This did not alter the appearance of the gun barrel since the flamethrower system had been inserted inside the barrel. The tanks thus converted were shared out between A and C Companies, but did not receive distinctive markings. Therefore, during the fighting, it was complicated for the infantry accompanying the tanks to identify the specialized vehicles. After the battle, the commanding officer of the 1st Battalion, 23rd Marines, recommended that "the flame thrower tanks have a distinctive marking so that they could be recognized [by supporting infantry]."

An aerial view of two late-production M4A2s on Tinian. Both belonged to B Company which did not copy the number of its tanks on the turret as it had done for Saipan. We can see *Gung Ho II* (bottom) and *Goldbrick Jr.* (top). (NARA)

Name-number association of the 4th Tank Battalion on Iwo Jima					
	HQ section	1st Platoon	2nd Platoon	3rd Platoon	4th Platoon
A Company	1	5 *The Ait Ball*	8 *Asiatic*	11	14
	2	6 *Applejack*	9 *Amazon*	12	15 *Ashland*
	3	7	10 *Alley-Oop*	13 *Ape*	16 *Astro*
			no number *Aflamo*[a]		
	4-F *Amen*[b]	-	-	no number	-
	no number (M32B3)	-			-
B Company	17 *Beelzebub*	20A *Bed Bug*	23	26 *Bouncer*	29 *Butch*[c]
	18	21 *Blackjack*	24 *Bugaboo*	27 *Bronco*	30 *Betty*
	19 *Boomerang*	22	25	28 *Bunny*[c]	31 *Bandit*[c]
	32 (M32B3)	-			-
C Company	33 *Cyclone*	37 *Cobra*	41 *Cairo*	44 *Crispy*	47 *Clodhopper*
	34 *Cyanide*[b]	38 *Comet*	42 *Calcutta*	45 *Cleaver*	48 *Clangor*
	35 *Cyclops*[d]	39 *The Count*	43 *Cape Town*	46 *Cracker*	49 *Couger*
	36 *Cyuzie*	40 *Coed*[a]	-	-	50 *Cleo*[a]
	51 *Cassie* (M32B3)	-	-	-	-

(NB. a name missing next to a number means it was not known)

a). Flamethrower tank b). Flail tank c). Name-number association uncertain d). Tankdozer

After the Marianas were captured, the 4th Tank Battalion abandoned the lively color markings on the turret roofs, as a tank commander of C Company explained: "We painted the top of the tanks when we went to Saipan. We painted them with yellow … and unfortunately that was an X mark for all the Japanese gunners [sic. observers positioned hilltop] … they just zeroed in on us … So we quit that very quickly …"

In A Company, the name *Assaulter* has been identified, but its number is unknown. The crew tended to play on the name's spelling, which was very close to "ass-salter" when pronounced.

Finally, the crews were in the habit of painting a clock on the rear of a tank—generally on the rear fording kit, near the liaison telephone, so as to help the infantry direct the tanks' fire at the targets. This clock, designated the "Target Clock," was painted yellow.

This photo was taken in the camp of the 3rd Tank Battalion on Guam after the battle of Iwo Jima. We can see the tank *Aflamo* from A Company, 4th Tank Battalion. It is one of the eight M4A3s converted into flamethrowers by the combined teams of the USMC, the Navy, and the U.S. Army before Iwo Jima. It has no number as it was received rather late. It was given to the 3rd Tank Battalion towards the end of the campaign since the unit had no large-capacity flame-throwing tanks. (Michael P. Hogan)

M4 TANKS OF THE 4TH MARINE TANK BATTALION, 1944

M4A2 (mid-production), *Bacchus*, 2nd Platoon, A Company, Saipan, June 1944.

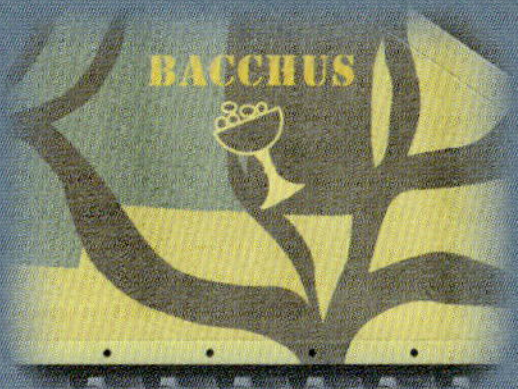

M4A2 (late), *Gremlin IV*, 3rd Platoon, B Company, Saipan, June 1944 (see also page 149, figure 4).

M4A2 (mid-production), *King Kong*, 3rd Platoon, C Company, Saipan, June 1944.

M4 AND M5 TANKS OF THE 4TH MARINE TANK BATTALION 1944–1945

M4A2 (mid-production), *Ace*, 1st Platoon, A Company, Tinian, July 1944.

M5A1, *Nannie*, 2nd Platoon, D Company, Tinian, July 1944.

M4A2 (late), flail tank, No. 4-F, *Amen*, HQ Platoon, A Company, Iwo Jima, February 1945.

Above: The Command Post of C Company, 4th Tank Battalion, on Iwo Jima. On the right we can see *Clodhopper* 47 and *Cleo* 50. In the center, the M4A3 *Doris* 53 was the battalion commander's tank. The tank battalion no longer had D Companies in 1945. (USMC HD)

Left and below: This color photo taken from a 1945 film on Iwo Jima shows M4A3 (75) W *Bugaboo* from B Company. Having noted the beneficial effects of wooden side protection, A and B Companies decided to do the same thing for Iwo Jima. Note also the tank track links welded onto the glacis and the turret for the same reason. The photo below shows the detail of the markings applied only to the right-hand part of the gun barrel. (NARA)

A photo taken on Hawaii showing an M4A3 (75) W from B Company being given its name. *Bunny* was the nickname of the tank commander's wife. After the Mariana campaign, the naming system for the tanks was rethought in the 4th Tank Battalion. The first letter of the tank's name was now the company's letter. Note that the UNIS marking has also changed its format. It denotes that the tank battalion was detached from the Division HQ to become a complete entity. Therefore, the 9 indicates the tanks, the 1 refers to the battalion (a single one within the division), and the 3 for B Company. The numbering of the UNIS marking varied from one division to another. (NARA via Ed. Gilbert)

Above: *Bed Bug* from B Company on Iwo Jima. The name, the UNIS number, and that of the tank were painted in yellow. The meaning of the letter A next to the tank number is a mystery. (USMC HD)

Left and below: *Ashland* 15 and *Asiatic* 8 both belonged to A Company which did not paint the UNIS marking on its tanks. Note that the lateral protection is made of plywood. In the case of *Ashland*, it was cut out of three detachable sections covering the flank and lined with concrete. (NARA/Author)

M4 TANKS OF THE 4TH MARINE TANK BATTALION, 1945

M4A3 75 (W), No. 10, *Alley-Oop*, 2nd Platoon, A Company, Iwo Jima, February 1945.

M4A3 75 (W), No. 24, *Bugaboo*, 2nd Platoon, B Company, Iwo Jima, February 1945.

M4A3 75 (W), tankdozer, No. 35, *Cyclops*, HQ Platoon, C Company, Iwo Jima, February 1945.

Above: Comet 38 was a standard M4A3 75 (W) from C Company. Unlike the other tanks in this unit, the name and the number were painted white. The slogan *Widow Maker* from the former tank *Illustrious* is seen painted in yellow on the gun barrel. (NARA)

Below left: Another example of a Sherman from C Company, *Cape Town* 43 had driven over a 500 kg bomb converted into a mine on the second airfield on Iwo Jima. The resulting explosion killed the whole crew except the tank commander. (Collection of Sergeant Major Bert R. Nave)

Below right: *Crispy* 44 belonged to 3rd Platoon, C Company. It was commanded by Lieutenant Gearl M. English. The tank number has been repeated on the fording kit but not the name. (NARA via Steve McCloud)

Above: The former M4A2 tankdozer from C Company, *Joker II*, was converted into a flail tank and rechristened *Cyanide* on Iwo Jima. (NARA via Steve Zaloga)

Left: Rear view of *Calcutta* 42 from 2nd Platoon, C Company. The name has been painted on the Stuart's reservoir used for transporting water for the infantry, as well as on the fording kit. On the side of the latter, we can clearly see the "Target Clock" painted for the infantry. "Phone" has been painted in white on the box containing the tank–infantry telephone. (NARA)

Below: A second tank was converted into a flail tank and used by A Company. The flail devices of *Cyanide* and *Amen* were destroyed during the landing on Iwo Jima and were never used. Note the camouflage made of large, sand-colored blotches on a dark olive-drab background on the *Amen*. (NARA)

Above and below: Photos taken from a 1945 color film showing *Betty* 30 from the 4th Platoon, B Company. The tank has all the standard markings of the 4th Tank Battalion on Iwo Jima. The crew chose the name because it sounded all-American. (USMC HD)

Above: The name and the number of the tank were traditionally painted on the rear of the fording kit. Here, the crew of the M4A3 *Amazon* from A Company is having a break on Iwo Jima. The number 9 is hidden by one of the crewmen. (Author's Collection)

Right: The number and the name of the tank were painted yellow on the rear of the fording kit of the tanks of the 4th Tank Battalion. Here, the M4A3 No. 16 *Astro* was lying on aerodrome number 2 of Iwo Jima. It is interesting to note the "Target Clock" on the kit. The tanks tended to draw sustained fire with dramatic results for the accompanying infantry. Note the bodies of the Marines on the ground. (NARA via Scott Freund)

Cassie was the recovery vehicle in C Company. It bore the number 51 painted in the center of the left-hand side armor plate. It is interesting to note the UNIS marking (914, painted in the half-moon), which was unusual for this unit. White factory markings are still visible below the vehicle's name. (Collection of Sergeant Major Bert R. Nave)

Cyclone was the Sherman belonging to Major Robert Neiman, C Company's commanding officer. Note the yellow markings. (USMC HD and USC)

9

The 5th Tank Battalion

Set up in January 1944 on the West Coast of the United States, the 5th Tank Battalion was sent to Hawaii in mid-August to improve its training. It took part in the battle of Iwo Jima in February and March 1945.

After Japan surrendered, the battalion was sent to Yokosuka and Sasebo for occupation duty from September 1945 to January 1946.

Iwo Jima (February–March 1945)

The three companies of the 5th Tank Battalion were identified by three different geometric shapes: A Company by a square, B Company by a circle, and C Company by a diamond.

Two figures were painted inside the shape with the first, from 1–6, indicating which platoon the vehicle belonged to: from 1–4 for the first four platoons, 5 for the replacement vehicles,[21] and 6 for the HQ Platoon.

The second number indicated the position of the tank within the platoon, with 0 for the platoon leader, 1 and 2 for the other two vehicles in the platoon.

Each company was, in theory, made up of five platoons of three M4A3 tanks. One of the tanks in the HQ Platoon was fitted with a bulldozer blade and recovery vehicles based on the M4 chassis also came into use.

Four additional M4A3s were converted into flamethrowers and assigned to the battalion before the fighting on Iwo Jima.

[21] The replacement vehicles were nonetheless part of the HQ Platoon. A Company was the only company to have one.

A photo taken from a 1945 film showing an M4A3 75 (W) from B Company. We can see the company circle painted yellow on the glacis. The tank bears the number 22, indicating that it belonged to the 2nd Platoon. We can see clearly the earth-colored blotches used to camouflage the vehicle. The sides are protected by corrugated steel plates, lined here with concrete. Finally, we can see the red tip of the aerial identification triangle on the roof of the turret. (USMC HD and USC)

Above: Unlike the other USMC units, the 5th Tank Battalion used geometric shapes to differentiate its companies and not the platoons. Square 61 *Davy Jones* was the command tank of Captain Jones of A Company. The camouflage consisted of large, cream-colored blotches painted over the Marine Corps green. (NARA via Kenneth Esters)

Left: Despite the mediocre quality of this image, we can see the circle identifying B Company at the rear of the M32B3 and the number 62 inside. The 60 series indicated the HQ Platoon. (USMC HD)

These tanks were identified by the letter F followed by a number from 1–4. The tanks F1 and F2 belonged to the HQ Platoon of A Company; F3 and F4 to the HQ Platoon of C Company.

Below: Diamond F3 was one of the two large-capacity flamethrowers of C Company. The nickname *Hot Rod* can be read on the gun barrel. (USMC HD)

Bottom: B Company's tankdozer landing from LST-141 on February 19, 1945. We can barely see the circle on the glacis of the vehicle with the number 63. This photograph is interesting in that it shows the white contour of the aerial identification triangle painted on the top of the turret. The aim of having a white edge was to make the marking even more visible from the sky. (USMC HD)

Note that the F1 and F2 flamethrowers were the only tanks in the battalion not to bear the geometric markings. Instead, the tactical call sign of the vehicle was painted in big yellow characters on the flanks and the rear of the vehicles (see the profile on page 131).

The tactical markings were painted white, cream, or yellow on the four sides of the tank's hull. However, some variations were observed, like on the front of the tank. B and C Companies tended to paint the tactical markings on the left-hand part of the glacis and A Company painted them on either side of the transmission block.

The disadvantage of the markings of the 5th Tank Battalion was that they were too small (except for F1 and F2, *cf.* profile), which made them difficult to read at a distance. Furthermore, the infantry did not know the system of markings the tanks used, making identifying the special tanks difficult. A flamethrower tank commander testifies:

"Identification was good for tank personnel but our infantry was lacking in knowledge as to what flame tanks were, or how to identify them. In other words, if our infantry knew our identification and our disposition they could save themselves a lot of trouble when they want to communicate with regular tanks by knowing which are flame tanks and which are regular tanks."[22]

The battalion also adopted tactical markings for aerial identification: a red equilateral triangle was painted on the roof of the turret; it was pointing forwards or backwards. In some cases, the triangle was edged with white to make it more visible from the air. This enabled aerial reconnaissance to identify the front line easily. Finally, the vehicles were often (but not systematically) given a name. Within A Company, the tank's name was painted white on the sides of the hull, next to the tactical marking.

According to historian Leife Hubert, C Company had given a sequence of three letters to each of its platoons, as the initial letter of its tanks' names. Thus the letters A, B, and C were assigned to the HQ Platoon (*Avenger* 62 [tankdozer], *Calamity* 63); the letters D–F to the 1st Platoon (*Earbanger* 11, *Dear Mom* 10), G–I for the 2nd Platoon (*Hobo* 21), J–L for the 3rd Platoon (*Jeannie, Killer, Lucky*), and M–O for 4th Platoon (*Moonshine* 42, *Nitemare* 40).

22 As the flame-throwing mechanism was directly incorporated into the barrel of a normal M4A3, the flame-throwing tank could not be differentiated from a standard tank, from the outside.

M4 TANKS OF THE 5TH MARINE TANK BATTALION, 1945

M4A3 75 (W), Square 42, *Iron Coffin*, 4th Platoon, A Company, Iwo Jima, February 1945.

M4A3 75 (W), modified into a flamethrower, HQ Platoon, A Company, Iwo Jima, February 1945.

M4A3 75 (W), Circle 61, HQ Platoon, B Company, Iwo Jima, February 1945.

Above: Square 21 was an M4A3 75 (W) belonging to 2nd Platoon, A Company. The tactical markings, as well as the name *Cyclone*, were painted white. We can see an additional armor plate between the hull and the planks, towards the front of the glacis. This shows that the tank had a small-capacity flamethrower (E-4-5 model) in the place of the hull machine gun which could be used by the assistant driver. (USMC HD)

Right: A famous photograph of Square 52 *Tokyo Express*, bogged down in volcanic ash on Iwo Jima. The tactical markings are painted white, except for the name, which is yellow. On the turret roof, a practiced eye would manage to see the aerial identification triangle covering the air intake, pointing rearwards. The (red) marking is not surrounded with white and is less visible on the photos. (USMC HD)

Known A Company tank names on Iwo Jima	
Tank Number	Name
61	*Davy Jones*
52	*Tokyo Express*
10	*Atlas*
12	*Scorpion*
21	*Cyclone*
?	*Horrible Hank*
42	*Iron Coffin*
31	*King Cobra*
32	*Rattler*
20	*Thunderbolt*
11 ?	*Icy Ducy*

The two flamethrowers were christened *The Five Aces* (F3) and *Torch* (F4).

Initially painted on the hull sides, the name was moved after the sides were covered with planks up to the crown of the turret, on the right- or left-hand side. B Company does not seem to have painted any names on its tanks, although in some rare cases, a name was painted on the gun barrel.

Finally, besides the tactical markings allowing the companies to be identified, another way of distinguishing them was to analyze the modifications made to the tank.

As well as covering the tank sides with planks, A Company also added planks to the suspension system to prevent Japanese soldiers from throwing explosive charges at them. The tank hatches were all covered with spikes.

The sides of B Company's tanks were covered with corrugated steel plates and the access hatches were surmounted with a frame on which chicken wire netting or pierced steel plates were attached.

C Company put spikes on the turret hatch and chicken wire cages on the hull hatches. Wooden planks also protected the flanks.

Occupying Japan (1945–1946)

In Japan, the 5th Tank Battalion kept its old M4A3s from which all the extra protection (wood, tank track links, spikes, cages, etc.) was taken off. The former tactical markings were covered over with paint and large two-figure numbers were

Above: The markings of this Company C Sherman consist of a diamond bearing the number 21 inside, painted on the glacis next to the gun travel lock, above the roller bearing. We can guess the name *Hobo* as well as a face on the cheek of the turret. (NARA via Jon Bernstein)

Below: The markings on the side of this M4A3 75 (W) have been done with chalk, a short while before the photo was taken, towards the end of the battle of Iwo Jima. The original markings consisted of a shape-number association defining the company, the platoon, and the position of the tank. Behind the word "via," we can faintly see a diamond; inside is the number 40. This indicates that this is a Sherman from C Company, 4th Platoon, the platoon leader's tank. The same marking was painted on the glacis behind the frame of the left-hand headlight of the Sherman. (NARA via Morgan Gillard)

painted on the flanks of the hull and the turret. There is little information as to what they meant. The numbers 30 (standard tank, A Company), 74 (flamethrower tank) and 50 (flamethrower tank) were the only ones to be identified.

Some tanks were also converted into POA-CWS-H5 flamethrowers with a 75 mm cannon and a barrel projecting the flaming liquid. These conversions were realized and planned for the invasion, before Japan capitulated.

Right: A rear view of Diamond 11 *Earbanger* from C Company. The tank bears interesting markings on its fording kit. On the left we can see the "Target Clock" with the inscription "Gun Target." On the right, the inscription "Put the phone back" with an arrow directed towards the bolted box above the track, encouraging the liaison telephone user to put it back. (NARA via Morgan Gillard)

Below: Two Shermans from B Company on Iwo Jima. This unit was the only one to use corrugated iron to protect the sides of its tanks from magnetic mines. The metal was not systematically painted as we can see on the left-hand tank. On this vehicle, the circle containing the tank number is painted in yellow and is barely legible on the metal, vertically above the first bogey. (NARA via Morgan Gillard)

M4 TANKS OF THE 5TH MARINE BATTALION, 1945

M4A3 75 (W), Diamond 11, *Earbanger*, 1st Platoon, C Company, February 1945.

M4A3 75 (W), modified as a flamethrower, HQ Platoon, C Company, Iwo Jima, February 1945.

POA-CWS-H5, No. 74, Sasebo, Japan, September 1945.

Above: POA-CWS-H5 flamethrowers of the 5th Tank Battalion in the process of destroying Japanese aircraft in the port of Sasebo in 1945. The vehicle which is farthest away bears the number 74. (Ed Gilbert)

Left: Diamond 41 from C Company had a camouflage made of three shades of light and dark olive drab, as well as cream-colored blotches. The tactical markings were painted in white, which made reading them easier than if they'd been painted in yellow. (NARA via Morgan Gillard)

Left: The tactical markings have not been repeated on the transmission block of this M4A3 from the 5th Tank Battalion. The name *Atlas* and the tactical marking Square 10 are however visible on the piece of wood on the ground (left). This is Lieutenant Stemkoski's tank; he commanded A Company's 1st Platoon. (USMC HD)

10

The 6th Tank Battalion

The 6th Tank Battalion was officially activated on Guadalcanal on October 1, 1944. It consisted of two experienced companies: the Tank Company, 4th Marines and Tank Company, 22nd Marines.

They were rechristened respectively A and B Companies, 6th Tank Battalion, when the new battalion was created. C Company was the last tank unit the USMC formed during the war. It was also a redesignation of the Tank Company, 29th Marines, activated in the United States on May 1, 1944. The 6th Tank Battalion took part in the fighting on Okinawa from April to June 1945. After Japan was defeated, the battalion was deployed at Tsingtao in China for maintaining order, until it was disbanded on March 26, 1946.

The 6th Marine Division to which the battalion was attached was disbanded in the summer of the same year. A rearguard unit—the 3rd Battalion, 4th Marines—was maintained in order to cover the troops reembarking, as communist pressure was getting stronger and stronger. The battalion was reinforced by a tank unit from the 6th Tank Battalion. Designated Tank Platoon, 3rd Battalion, 4th Marines, it consisted of seven vehicles: four standard M4A3 75 (W)s, a tankdozer, a flamethrower tank (probably the POA-CWS-H5 model), and an M32B3.

The unit was disbanded after most of the American troops were withdrawn from Tsingtao, in the fall of 1947.

A photograph taken from a color film showing M4A3s from the 6th Tank Battalion maneuvering. They have not yet been given their combat modifications. These Shermans belonged to A Company as indicated by the red of the tactical markings on the turret. The dark red seen in the photo was not easily visible on an olive background. The markings were redone before the landing on Okinawa and the red paint was mixed with white to obtain a lighter red, more visible at long distance. (USMC HD)

Okinawa (April–June 1945)

On Okinawa, the 6th Tank Battalion was made up of an H&S Company and three line companies (A, B, and C). The H&S Company was equipped with an M4A3 75 (W) command tank, an M32B3 recovery vehicle, four M4A3 75 (W) replacement tanks, and three reserve bulldozer blades to make up for the losses to come during the campaign.

The three line companies were made up of five platoons of three tanks each, i.e. 15 M4A3 75 (W)s per company, of which one was a tankdozer. An M32B3 also equipped the Maintenance Section from the HQ Platoon of each company.

Although the unit was only officially activated in October 1944, its organization started as early as the spring of 1944. On May 17, Lieutenant Colonel Robert L. Denig, Jr., commanding the battalion, drew up a memorandum in which he gave instructions concerning the markings of the battalion tanks.

Left: This photograph, taken at the beginning of the Okinawa campaign, shows an M4A3 from the 6th Tank Battalion with its initial protection against the antitank guns. The track links were only welded on the glacis and around the turret. The hull was protected by steel plates. The lack of equipment made the 6th Tank Battalion cut out squares of armor plating and place them on vulnerable points: the driver's and co-driver's posts, and the fuel tanks. (USMC HD)

Below: Diamond 2 and 3 on Naha airfield, Okinawa, 1945. The diamond indicates vehicles from the 3rd Platoon. The original photo caption indicates that the tanks belonged to B Company. Note the extra armor, made up of steel Sherman track links, welded on the sides during the campaign. (USMC HD)

Above: Although the colors are not visible in black-and-white photos, the presence of the fixations of the T6 kit enables us to associate this M4A3 to C Company. The tactical markings are therefore painted yellow. (USMC HD)

Left: This photo was taken in October 1952 in Nevada following nuclear tests. The vehicle is a tank from the 6th Tank Battalion, a veteran of Okinawa. This is the tank of the executive officer, Clover 2, probably from A Company, judging by the grayish shade of the tactical marking. Note the late USMC format 102501. (NARA)

The battalion used a color–shape–number sequence to identify its tanks. The three companies were identified by their colors. A Company had light-red markings,[23] B Company white, and C Company yellow.[24]

The platoons were identified by geometric shapes: a square for the 1st Platoon, a circle for the 2nd Platoon, a diamond for the 3rd Platoon, and a triangle for the 4th Platoon. The HQ Platoon was identified by a cloverleaf.

Inside each shape there was a number from 1–3 with 1 for the platoon commander and 3 for the platoon sergeant. Within the HQ Platoon, 1 designated the company commander, 2, the executive officer, and 3, the bulldozer tank.

Within battalion H&S Company, the tanks were identified by a white heart. Number 1 designated the commander's tank. Tanks 3, 4, 5, and 6 were replacement vehicles intended for compensating losses suffered in the battle.

The memorandum also stipulated where the markings were to be put:

> Large size Rear: (a) On the rear of the turret. (b) On the lower fording stack. Small size Side: To the rear of the turret, below the upright support for the engine hatches. Small size Front. In the upper right hand corner of the front slope plate. (Looking toward the front). The edge of the figure should be at the edge of the tank. And the top of the figure at the top of the slope plate.

[23] Originally, the markings were red, but on an olive-drab background they were not easily visible. The crews therefore mixed white paint with the red, making the color lighter, tending towards a pink. Officially however, the Marines designated this color as "light red."

[24] The company's 13 tanks were equipped with pontoons enabling them to float (T6 equipment). They were landed off Okinawa and "swum" by their own means to the shore.

Above: The bridges on Okinawa had not been built to take the Sherman's 32 tons. The tactical marking indicates that this is the executive officer of A or B Company. The cloverleaf (visible on the rear of the turret) is the insignia of the HQ Platoons. We can see the winged star intended for aerial identification on the roof of the turret. (NARA via Morgan Gillard)

Left: A photo taken from a 1945 film showing the camouflage scheme consisting of two shades of olive drab. The tactical marking of this M4A3 has been painted white, indicating that this was B Company. The triangle designates 4th Platoon and the 1, the platoon leader. (Oscar E. Gilbert)

Left: Square 2 from the 1st Platoon of C Company has driven over a mine which has blown off one of its bogeys. Despite the impressive nature of this type of damage, the company mechanics were capable of getting a vehicle back in shape after one or two days' work. (USMC HD)

Bottom: Command tank of the 4th Platoon, A Company, 6th Tank Battalion, on Okinawa. The tactical marking was painted light red. There is no doubt about the Texan origin of several crew members when we see the top of the turret of this M4A3 75 (W) decorated with cows' horns. (Bob Botts via Ed Gilbert)

Square 2 from B Company has driven over a 500 kg bomb converted into an antitank mine by the Japanese. The markings are white. (NARA via Morgan Gillard)

M4 TANKS OF THE 6TH TANK BATTALION, 1945

M4A3 75 (W), T6, Clover 2, HQ Platoon, C Company, Okinawa, April 1945.

M4A3 75 (W), Square 1, Tank Platoon, 3rd Battalion, 4th Marines, Tsingtao, January 1946.

Above: This photo taken in China shows the 6th Tank Battalion before an inspection. Behind the jeeps, we can see the tank of the battalion's commander, *Heart One*, as well as the M32B3 of the battalion HQ. The tactical markings were painted white at battalion level. (USMC HD)

Left: This M4A3 has recently landed on Oroku peninsula and still bears its fording kits. This image enables us to appreciate the modifications intended to protect it from antitank gunfire (welded steel track links) and explosives thrown into the suspension system (horizontal steel bars on the bogeys). Note also the presence of the liaison telephone above the left-hand track. (USMC HD)

The tank of the platoon sergeant of 1st Platoon, B Company, supported the 22nd Marines as they advanced on Naha in May 1945. The simplified USMC emblem has been applied using a stencil under the white tactical marking. (NARA via Morgan Gillard)

In the field, a large geometric shape has been added on the front part of the hull sides to make identification easier.

Finally, the white five-point stars were painted on the turret roofs of all the tanks for aerial recognition.

Tank Platoon, 3rd Battalion, 4th Marines

The markings on the vehicles of the tank platoon consisted of large, solid squares, painted white with a number from 1–7, in olive drab on the inside.

The square was painted at the top on the left corner of the glacis, on the hull sides, towards the front of the tank and probably on the rear of the turret.

Conclusion

The diversity of the USMC markings—both simple and complex—made them unique during World War II.

Today they are a source of curiosity, interest, and inspiration for history or modeling buffs. The markings' variety ceased at the end of the 1940s when the system was standardized. This was adopted originally by B Company of the 2nd Tank Battalion in 1943 and improved during the Mariana campaign in the summer of 1944: the company letter followed by two numbers (first, the platoon and second, the position of the tank in the platoon). This system of tactical markings lasted until 2021 when the USMC decided to get rid of its tanks, once and for all.

An M4A3 (105) from the 1st Tank Battalion on Guam at the end of the 1940s. Note the now harmonized letter-number system used to identify the company, the platoon, and the position of the tank. The battalion is indicated by a number painted within a little yellow diamond, halfway along the side of the Sherman. (NARA)

Appendix 1

Theoretical Structure and Organization of the Marine Corps Units

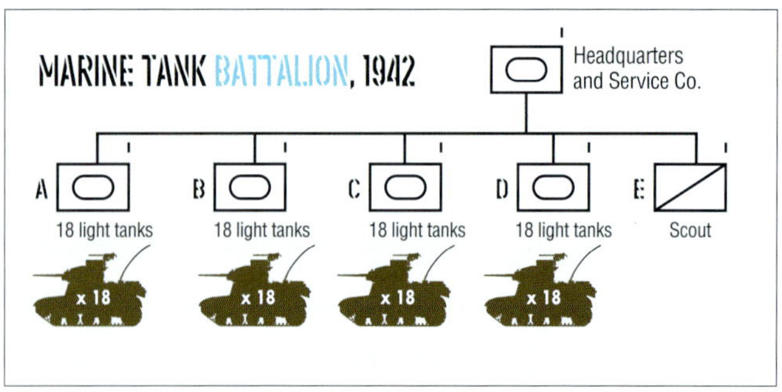

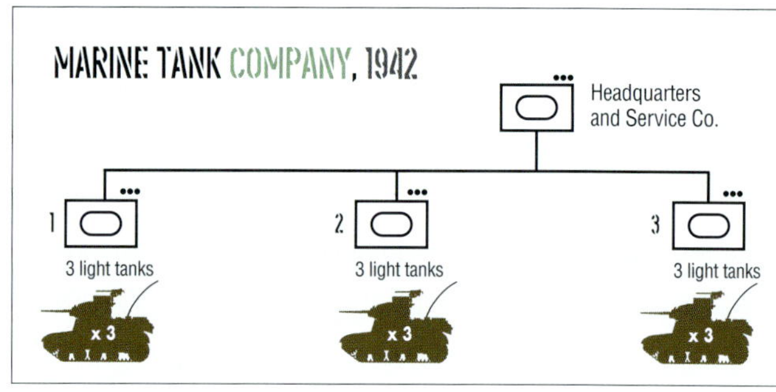

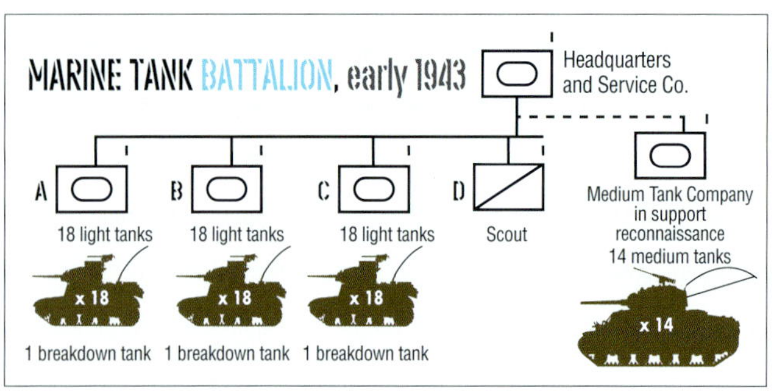

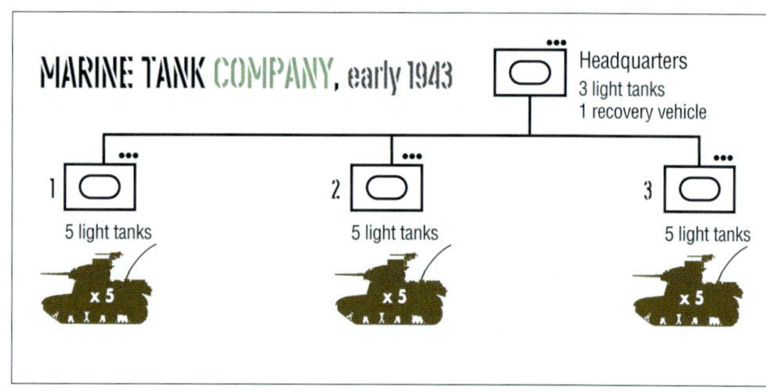

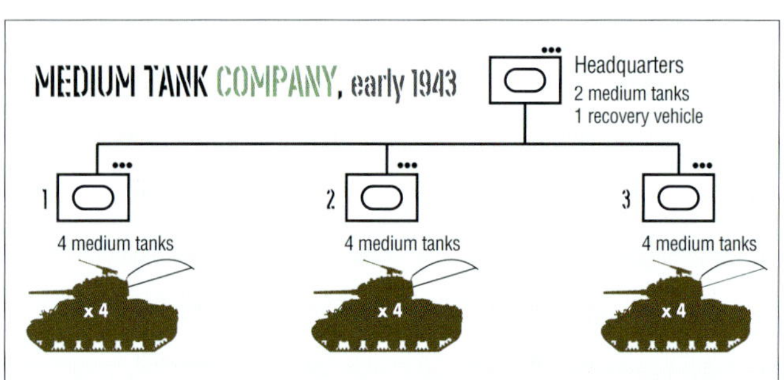

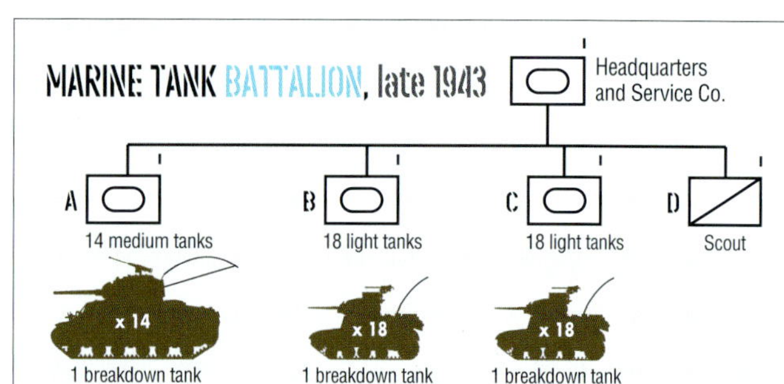

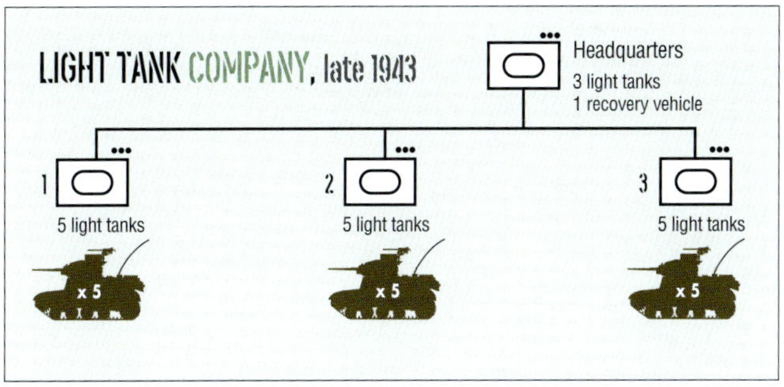
LIGHT TANK COMPANY, late 1943
Headquarters
3 light tanks
1 recovery vehicle
1
5 light tanks
x 5
2
5 light tanks
x 5
3
5 light tanks
x 5

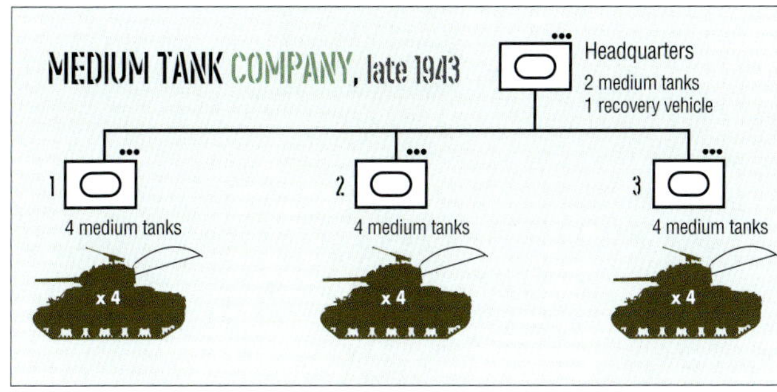
MEDIUM TANK COMPANY, late 1943
Headquarters
2 medium tanks
1 recovery vehicle
1
4 medium tanks
x 4
2
4 medium tanks
x 4
3
4 medium tanks
x 4

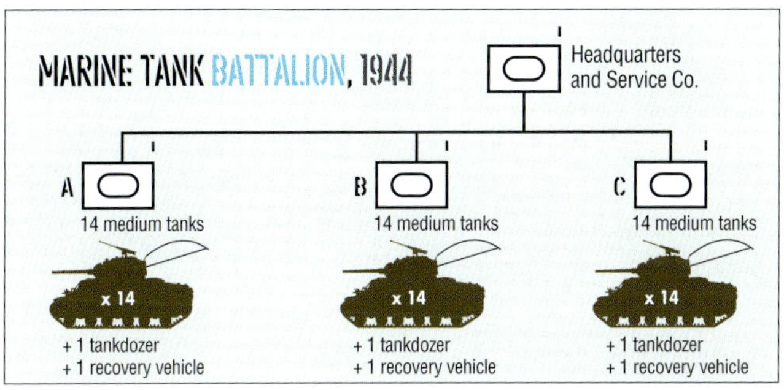
MARINE TANK BATTALION, 1944
Headquarters
and Service Co.
A
14 medium tanks
x 14
+ 1 tankdozer
+ 1 recovery vehicle
B
14 medium tanks
x 14
+ 1 tankdozer
+ 1 recovery vehicle
C
14 medium tanks
x 14
+ 1 tankdozer
+ 1 recovery vehicle

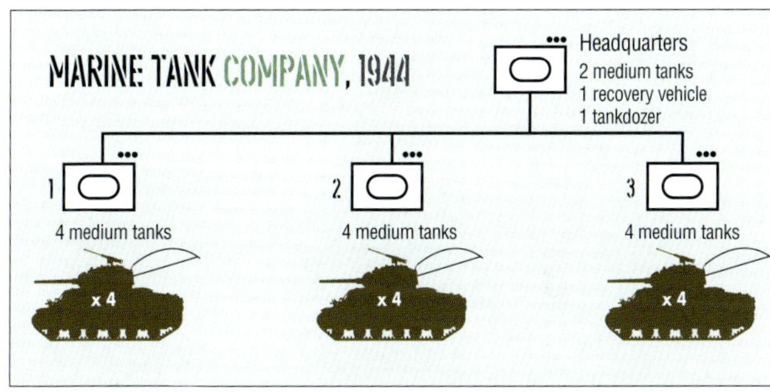
MARINE TANK COMPANY, 1944
Headquarters
2 medium tanks
1 recovery vehicle
1 tankdozer
1
4 medium tanks
x 4
2
4 medium tanks
x 4
3
4 medium tanks
x 4

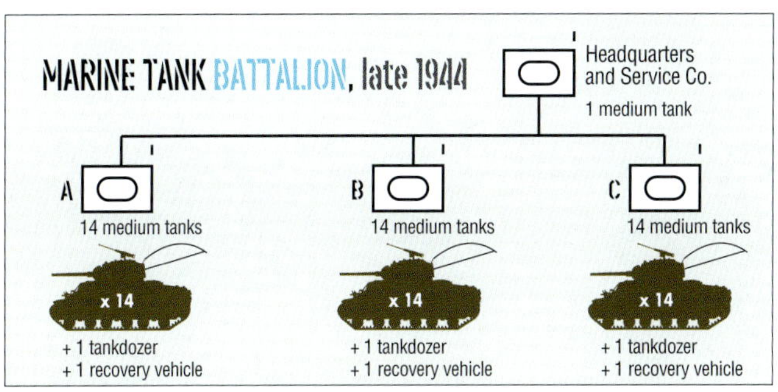
MARINE TANK BATTALION, late 1944
Headquarters
and Service Co.
1 medium tank
A
14 medium tanks
x 14
+ 1 tankdozer
+ 1 recovery vehicle
B
14 medium tanks
x 14
+ 1 tankdozer
+ 1 recovery vehicle
C
14 medium tanks
x 14
+ 1 tankdozer
+ 1 recovery vehicle

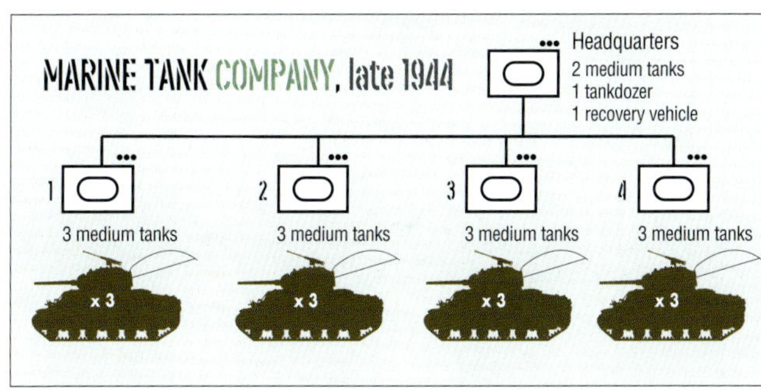
MARINE TANK COMPANY, late 1944
Headquarters
2 medium tanks
1 tankdozer
1 recovery vehicle
1
3 medium tanks
x 3
2
3 medium tanks
x 3
3
3 medium tanks
x 3
4
3 medium tanks
x 3

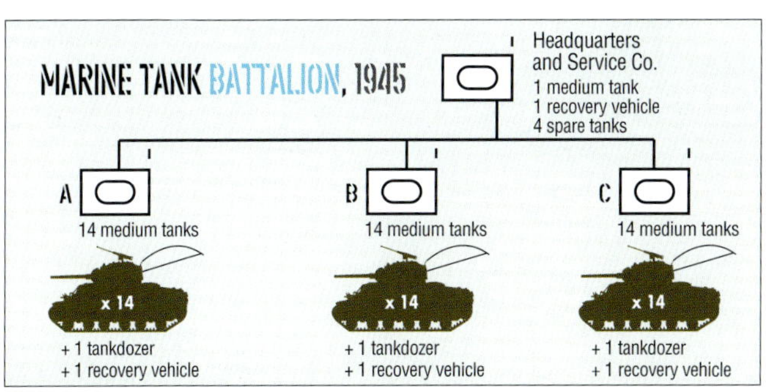
MARINE TANK BATTALION, 1945
Headquarters
and Service Co.
1 medium tank
1 recovery vehicle
4 spare tanks
A
14 medium tanks
x 14
+ 1 tankdozer
+ 1 recovery vehicle
B
14 medium tanks
x 14
+ 1 tankdozer
+ 1 recovery vehicle
C
14 medium tanks
x 14
+ 1 tankdozer
+ 1 recovery vehicle

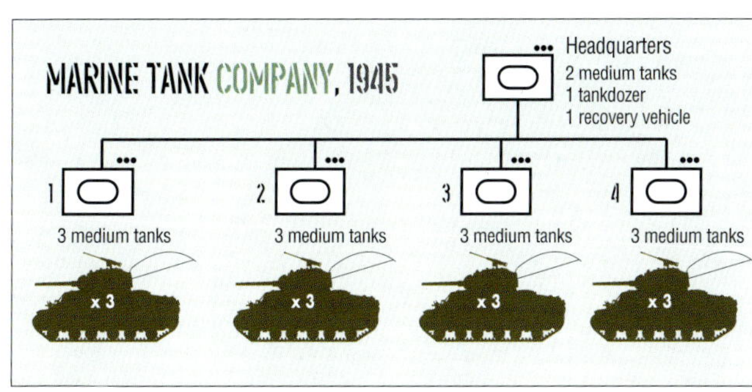
MARINE TANK COMPANY, 1945
Headquarters
2 medium tanks
1 tankdozer
1 recovery vehicle
1
3 medium tanks
x 3
2
3 medium tanks
x 3
3
3 medium tanks
x 3
4
3 medium tanks
x 3

Appendix 2

Markings Intended for Aerial Observation 1943–1945

1

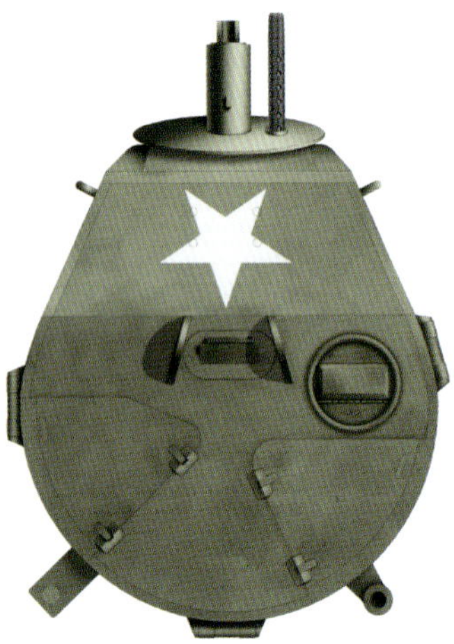

2

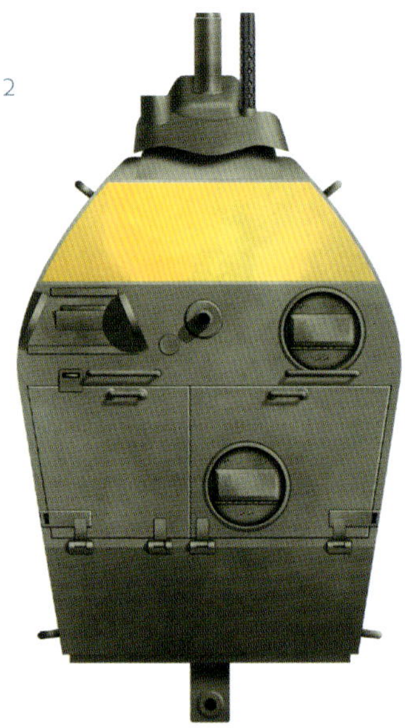

1. White star on the turret of the light Stuart tanks. A marking used by C Company, 2nd Tank Battalion, on Tarawa in 1943, by B Company, 4th Tank Battalion, in the Marshall Islands, on the M3A1 Satans (illustrated), and the M5A1 from D Company, 2nd Tank Battalion, in the Marianas in 1944.

2. Roof covered with yellow paint on Stuart M3A1 Satans and M5A1 tanks (illustrated) of the 4th Tank Battalion in the Marianas in June–July 1944.

3

4

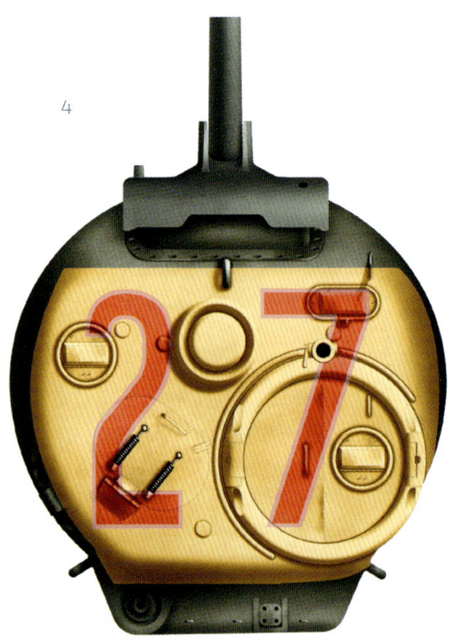

3 and 4. Roof covered with yellow paint (exceptionally orange) of the M4A2s of the 4th Tank Battalion in the Marianas in June–July 1944.

3. Version of the yellow roof used by A and C Companies.

4. Yellow roof with a number used by B Company.

5

6

5. Five-point star used on the M4A2s of the 2nd Tank Battalion during the Mariana campaign in June and July 1944. Also used by B Company, 1st Tank Battalion, at Peleliu in 1944, the 2nd Tank Battalion in 1945, and the 6th Tank Battalion on Okinawa in 1945.

6. Winged star used by the 3rd Tank Battalion, the Tank Company, 22nd Marines, and probably the Tank Company, 4th Marines, on Guam in 1944. Reused by the 3rd Tank Battalion on Iwo Jima in 1945. Employed on several tanks of the 6th Tank Battalion on Okinawa.

7

8

7. and 8. Red triangle, sometimes edged with white, used by the 5th Tank Battalion on the turret of its M4A3s on Iwo Jima, in 1945.

Appendix 3

History of the Marine Corps' Armored Arm

At the end of World War I, the tank was unanimously recognized as an indispensable weapon on the battlefield. This did not escape the USMC which, during the inter-war period, was striving to set itself up and survive the budgetary restrictions imposed by peacetime.

The USMC found its salvation in the U.S. Navy. Both of them had already anticipated a conflict in the Pacific against the Empire of the Rising Sun which did not conceal its expansionist ambitions. Therefore, on a battlefield covering a fifth of the world, and 98 percent of which consisted of water, the American fleet had to have rear bases so it could stock up with fresh supplies on its way to its objective: Formosa (nowadays Taiwan). The USMC teams led by Major Earl H. Ellis did indeed envisage a conflict in the Pacific, and identified Formosa as the rallying point of the American fleet. At the beginning, this would follow two axes: the South West Pacific axis and the Central

The first tanks bought by the USMC were these M1917s. They were sent to Tientsin in China at the end of the 1920s but were not used in combat. (NARA via Ken Estes)

The tanks which the USMC could use during the 1930s were limited in size and weight by the ships' cranes and the boats available. Undeniably, at the time, there were no barges designed for landing a vehicle on a beach. We see here the test carried out at the end of the 1930s to load a small Marmon-Herrington CTL-3 tank onto a Navy boat using ramps. (NARA via Ken Estes)

Pacific axis which would converge on Formosa before turning towards the main islands of Japan. Entitled "712H Operation Plan: Advanced Base Operations in Micronesia," and published in 1921, this work was considered by historians as prophetic: it described with stunning precision the way events would unfold and turn out only two decades later.

Thus, the bigger islands and smaller islands spread around the Pacific would be ideal bases, which it would be useful to take and defend against the enemy. The U.S. Navy thus worked closely with the USMC in order to make it a specialist in amphibious operations. Numerous career officers of the USMC were veterans of fighting in World War I. They very quickly saw a parallel between a shore held by the Japanese enemy and the German trenches where only tanks had proved how useful they were as a penetration weapon, able to break through the lines.

As a result, a beach bitterly defended by the enemy could only be neutralized with armored support.

The idea made its way throughout the various USMC echelons. On December 5, a platoon of three M1917 tanks (French FT Renaults, but produced in the United States) borrowed from the U.S. Army was hastily set up to take part in the Navy's winter exercises. They were used in a defensive role during the maneuvers, and not with the initial purpose of breakthrough.

Indeed, a major technical problem prevented the tank from developing rapidly as an offensive arm within the USMC: the U.S. Navy did not have any boats able to disembark these vehicles onto a beach. Ways around this problem were found by adapting ramps on conventional boats but the system was a long way from being satisfactory.

Nonetheless, the USMC managed to obtain up to eight M1917s which were sent to China in 1927 to defend the Shanghai and Peking trading posts during the civil war which was becoming increasingly important.

The platoon of light tanks was finally repatriated in 1928 and left in abeyance.

The USMC, still convinced that armor was useful, in 1935 decided to consult industrialists for a design of a tank light enough to make up for the lack of specific boats, and above all, which could be hoisted aboard the boats by the ships' cranes, whose lifting capacity was restricted.

The Marmon-Herrington Company responded favorably and designed the CTL-3 in 1936 respecting the weight requirements: 5 tons maximum. The vehicle therefore had no turret, was only armed with a machine gun, and only had quarter-inch (6.35 mm) armor.

Although the CTL-3 turned out to be fragile from a mechanical point of view, it was fast, agile, and easily maneuverable. It was impressive during the 1937 maneuvers, so the USMC asked the industrialists to improve it, resulting in the CTL-3A and CTL-6 versions in 1941.[25]

In 1938, the U.S. Navy designed a specific boat for landing the vehicles; it was fitted with a ramp.

The following year, the industrialist Andrew J. Higgins designed a barge with a shallow draught enabling it to approach the coast and then withdraw easily. Improved later with a ramp allowing a vehicle to be landed, this boat seemed more reliable than the Navy's, which were quickly abandoned. Higgins improved his barges and at the beginning of the 1940s, designed the LCM-1 or the Landing Craft Mechanized, which was able to transport and land the U.S. Army's 14-ton tanks, armed with a turret-mounted gun.

With the initial technical restrictions now removed, the USMC decided not to continue with Marmon-Herrington. The projects already in progress which gave rise to the CTM-3TBD (fitted with a turret but still with no cannon) in 1941 were carried out well but were not pursued.

Moreover, the geopolitical context (the war in Europe and unabated Japanese expansionism in Asia) incited the Marine Corps to find a tank able to respond to the needs of the emergency.

The U.S. Marine Corps made do with the U.S. Army's family of light tanks. The first vehicle, some M2A4s, arrived in 1940, and was followed in 1941 by the M3, an improved version of the M2.

Concerned with buying its new tanks quickly, the USMC did not look too closely at the engine. As a result, when the United States entered the war, several models fitted out with different engines equipped the first USMC tank units.

On the old continent, the Blitzkrieg showed that tanks equipped with 37 mm cannon and lightly armored were already obsolete and it was urgent for the U.S. Army to catch up. A tank fitted

25 The versions kept the initial characteristics of the CTL-3, but were re-engined and their suspension system was improved.

The tactical transport of the tanks onto the beaches, designed by the U.S. Army Ordnance Department, was made possible by the industrialist Andrew Higgins, who designed adapted landing barges. This LCM-3 lying off Saipan, carrying M4A2s from B Company, 4th Tank Battalion, has been hit by a Japanese shell. (NARA)

with a 75 mm cannon in the turret had to be designed quickly. After several years of research, the M4 Sherman medium tank saw the light of day in 1942. As with the light tanks, there were several versions with different engines (diesel or petrol).

With this information about the war in Europe, the USMC sought to get hold of medium tanks and obtained its first M4s in 1942. The first Sherman acquired was the M4A4 with a Chrysler petrol engine. At the beginning of 1943, the USMC received a version powered by a diesel engine. Faced with the complexity of maintaining the Chrysler petrol engine (consisting, in reality, of five car engines coupled together), the Corps turned towards the diesel version (only two lorry engines coupled together)[26] abandoned by the U.S. Army, which revealed servicing difficulties and reliability problems. The USMC had to be content with this: this was the model available in the greatest numbers and most quickly.[27]

The USMC equipped itself with medium tanks because it was no longer restricted by naval technology. The industrialist Higgins designed the LCM-3 in 1942, able to transport a 30-ton Sherman and land it on a beach. The lifting capacity of the ships' cranes had also been greatly increased and was no longer a restriction.

At the same time, the Marine Corps continued to receive M5A1 Stuart light tanks; it had placed orders for these before it knew how many of the Shermans it would be able to obtain, and when it would be able to obtain them.

With American production intensifying during the war and the production lines of M4A2 threatening to shut down, the U.S. Marine Corps was encouraged to equip itself with the M4A3 75 (W) from 1944 onwards. Finally in 1945, the 75 mm gun, which had equipped the Sherman from the beginning, was replaced either by the 76 mm cannon or by the 105 mm howitzer. The first was of no use against the type of defenses encountered in the Pacific theater of operations so the USMC opted for the second and obtained some M4A3 (105) in 1945.

The M4A3 75 (W)—being available in great numbers in 1945—had a handful of examples which had their main gun converted into a flamethrower (the POA-CWS-H1 version). Anticipating the invasion of Japan, an improved version was designed: the POA-CWS-H5 with both weapons (cannon and flamethrower) but, just like the M4A3 (105), this model did not take part in the fighting, because Japan capitulated on August 15, 1945.

26 The M4A4 version was not used in combat by the USMC. Only 22 examples were acquired.

27 Unlike the preconceived idea, the USMC did not choose the diesel engine because of its compatibility with the fuel used by the Navy's ships. Diesel and gasoline were both used by the U.S. Navy. The USMC made do with the version available at the time.

Appendix 4

USMC Campaigns in the Pacific

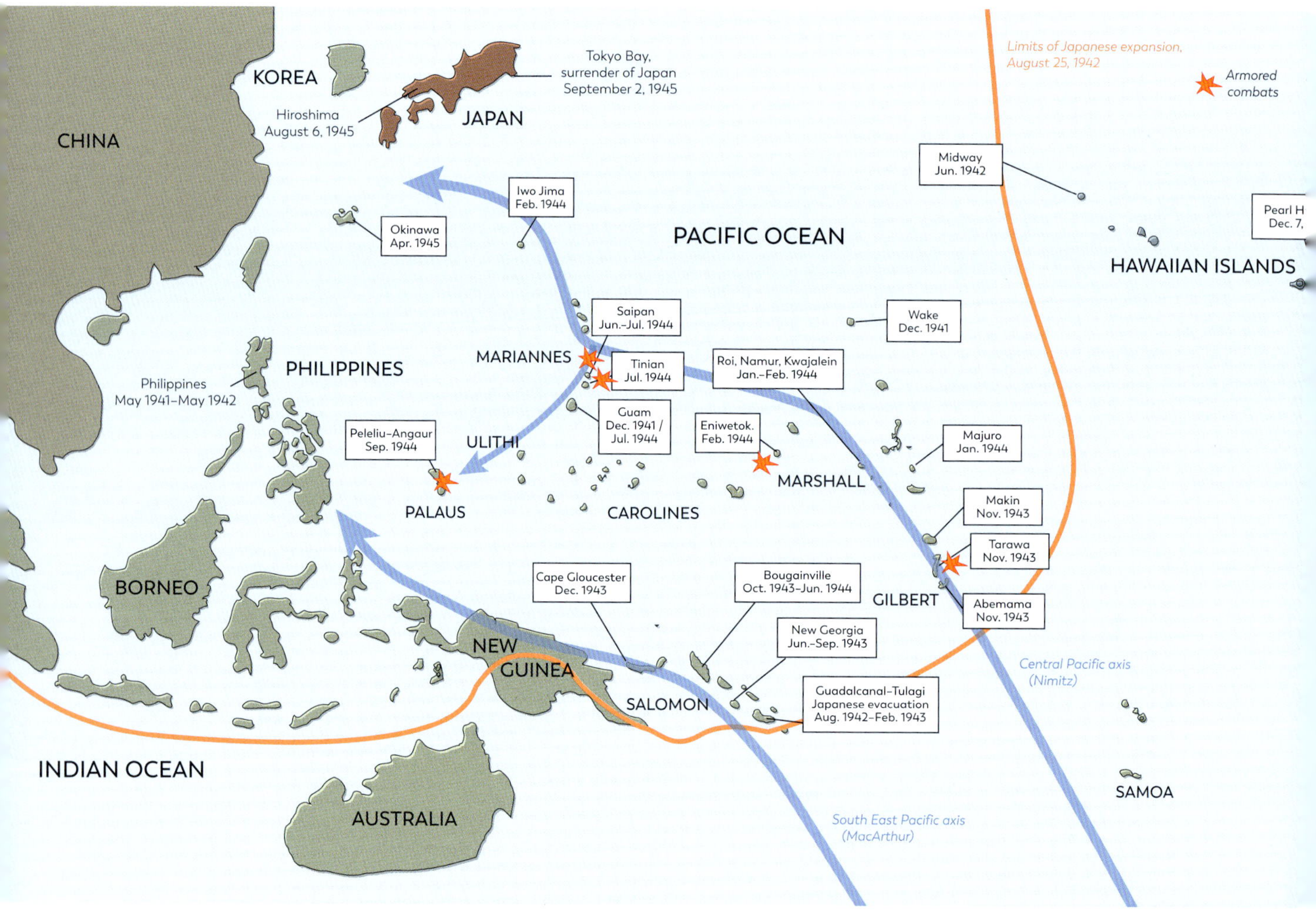

Bibliography

The documentation relating to the specific markings of the different U.S. Marine Corps tank units during World War II is relatively rare. Most of the directives taken at company or battalion level have either not been recorded or lost with time. The work thus presented in this book is based mainly on the study of period photographs and films. Reports on the fighting complete this analysis, the latter using (from time to time) references to the markings used on the tanks.

Finally, and above all, the interviews with veterans enabled us to reconstruct the gymnastics (sometimes complex) of several unit identification systems. As a result, the interviews conducted by Dr Oscar E. "Ed" Gilbert Jr., at the end of the 1990s and bequeathed to the author of this book, are a non-negligible source of details.

The first, and even secondhand, oral and written sources listed below have been used in this study.

Books and memoirs

Bellmon, Henry and Pat. *The Life and Times of Henry Bellmon.* U.S: Council Oak Publishing Co., 1992.

Boardman, Robert. *Unforgettable Men in Unforgettable Times.* U.S.: self-published, 1998.

Cansière, Romain. *Tanks on Iwo Jima 1945.* Oxford: New Vanguard 329, Osprey Publishing, 2024.

Cansière, Romain, and Oscar E. Gilbert. *USMC M4A2 Sherman vs Japanese Type 95 Ha-Go, The Central Pacific 1943–44.* Oxford: Duel 108, Osprey Publishing, 2021.

Estes, Kenneth W. *Marines Under Armor: The Marine Corps and the Armored Fighting Vehicle, 1916–2000.* Annapolis (MD, U.S.): Naval Institute Press, 2000.

Estes, Kenneth W. *US Marine Corps Tank Crewman 1941–1945.* Oxford: Warrior 92, Osprey Publishing, 2005.

Gilbert, Oscar E. *Marine Tank Battles In The Pacific.* U.S.: Combined Publishing, 2001.

Gilbert, Oscar E., and Romain Cansière. *Tanks in Hell, A Marine Corps Tank Company on Tarawa.* Philadelphia (U.S.): Casemate Publishers, 2015.

Giuliani, Raymond et al. *Sherman dans le Pacifique, 1943–1945,* Paris: Histoire & Collections, 2015 and reedition, 2023.

Harper, David E. *Tank Warfare on Iwo Jima.* U.S.: Squadron / Signal Publications, 2008.

Neiman, Robert M., and Kenneth W. Estes. *Tanks on the Beaches: A Marine Tanker in the Pacific War.* U.S.: Texas A & M University Press, 2003.

Yaffe, Bertram A. *Fragments of War: A Marine's Personal Journey.* U.S.: Naval Institute Press, 1999.

Zaloga, Steven J. *US Marine Corps Tanks of World War II.* Oxford: New Vanguard 186, Osprey Publishing, 2012.

Zaloga, Steven J. *US Marine Tanks in World War Two.* London: Tanks Illustrated 29, Arms & Armour Press Ltd., 1988.

Official Reports

4th Marine Division Operations Report. *Special Comments*. Annex E, 1944.

Bale, Edward L. *A Company, 2nd Tank Battalion Action Report*. Iheya–Aguni: 1945.

Bale, Edward L. *A Company, 2nd Tank Battalion Action Report*. Southern Okinawa: 1945.

Blake, Robert W. *Report of the Ninth Defense Battalion Tank Platoon's Operation in the New Georgia Area*. August 24, 1943.

Calcutt, Harry. *Report on Downside Operations*. February 26, 1944.

Calcutt, Harry. *Special Action Report of Tank Co. 22nd Marines on Guam*. March 30, 1945.

Collins, William R. *Action Report, Iwo Jima Operation*. February 19–March 26, 1945, 5th Tank Bn. April 24, 1945.

Commander, Eniwetok Expeditionary Group (CTG 51.11). *Report of Eniwetok Operation*. 1944.

Daily report. Unit No. 365. August 21, 1942.

Evans, H. H. *Special Action Report—Guam Operation*. April 19, 1945.

Evans, H. H. *3rd Tank Battalion Action Report (Iwo Jima)*. Enclosure H, April 9, 1945.

Gardelle, Lewis. *Observers Report on Forager Operation*. July 13, 1944.

McCoy, Charles W. *Special Action Report of the Second Tank Battalion*. December 14, 1943.

McCoy, Charles W. *Special Action Report, Tinian Operation*. August 14, 1944.

Milne, H. T. *Marking of Individual Tanks*. November 17, 1944.

Morell, Philip C. *Special Action Report of Tank Co. 4th Marines on Guam*. February 7, 1945.

Robillard, F. S. *Repainting Combat Vehicles*. September 22, 1941.

Roff, Edward G. *Special Action Report of Company "B," First Tank Battalion, from 9 January 1944 to 12 May 1944*. May 27, 1944.

Schmidt, R. K. *Iwo Jima, 4th Tank Battalion Report*. Annex Jig, May 30, 1945.

Schmidt, R. K. *Report of 4th Tank Battalion (Saipan)*. Annex K, August 20, 1944.

Schmidt, R. K. *Report of 4th Tank Battalion (Tinian)*. Annex K, August 22, 1944.

Smith, H. M. *Report of Flintlock Operations, 4th Tank Battalion*. April 29, 1944.

Special Action Report, Okinawa Nansei-Shoto, First Marine Division. (Rein), 1945.

Special Action Report, Okinawa Operation, Phases I and II, 6th Tank Battalion. May 29, 1945.

Special Action Report, Palau Operation, First Marine Division. (Rein), Annex J, Tanks, 1944.

Withers, H. J. *Special Action Report of Third Tank Battalion, Third Marine Division*. (Bougainville), August 18, 1944.

Interviews

Bryk, Clarence, Edward Bale, oral history interview OH00251. National Museum of the Pacific War, Fredericksburg, Texas: September 22, 2001.

Cansière, Romain, Gilbert, Oscar E., interview with Robert Falkenbury, September 6, 2018.

Cansière, Romain, interview with Arthur Russell, September 4, 2018.

Cansière, Romain, interview with Edward Gazel, September 3, 2018.

Cansière, Romain, interview with Jerry Ingram, March 3, 2019.

Cansière, Romain, interview with Martin Murphy, June 13, 2019.

Cansière, Romain, interview with Myron Czubko, September 2, 2018.

Cansière, Romain, interview with Robert Meier, December 4, 2018.

Gilbert, Oscar E., Cansière Romain, interview with Ed Bale, July 31, 2013.

Gilbert, Oscar E., Cansière Romain, interview with Joe Woolum, July 23, 2013.

Gilbert, Oscar E., interview with Charles B. Ash, December 1, 1998.

Gilbert, Oscar E., interview with Hal Rogers, November 23, 1998.

Gilbert, Oscar E., interview with Mike Shivetts, July 2, 2013.

Gilbert, Oscar E., interview with Philip Morell, November 5, 1998.

Gilbert, Oscar E., interview with Robert Botts, November 19, 1998.
Gilbert, Oscar E., interview with Robert Neiman, December 15, 1998.
Gilbert, Oscar E., interview with Rowland Hall, May 25, 1998.
Gilbert, Oscar E., interview with Vincent Young, October 30, 2000.
Gilbert, Oscar E., interview with William McMillian, May 25, 1998.

Articles

Ash, Charles B., "Letter to the editor." *Newsletter of the Marine Corps Tankers Association* Vol. 12, No. 2-01 (June 2001): 9.

Estes, Kenneth W., "Guadalcanal, 1st Tank Action!" *Newsletter of the Marine Corps Tankers Association* Vol. 12, No. 1-01, (March 2001): 16–18.

Gilbert, Oscar E., *Tactical and other Markings of U.S. Marine Corps Tank Units, 1941–1945*, unpublished, undated.

Hall, Rowland, "March Newsletter Surprise!" *Newsletter of the Marine Corps Tankers Association* Vol. 10, No. 299 (June 1999): 7.

Sledger, Joe, "A Unique Tank Platoon," *Newsletter of the Marine Corps Tankers Association* Vol. 10, No. 499 (December 1999): 5–6.

Wyatt, Whitlow et al., Newsletter *The Bogey Wheel* (unofficial publication of B Company, 2nd Tank Battalion), Issue Nos. 1–47 (1983–1998).

Acknowledgments

This book was started in 2013 and is the culmination of 10 years' research variously conducted from France and the United States to try and document the USMC tank markings used during World War II.

Directly or indirectly, a number of people have given me precious help in this historical reconstruction work.

Firstly, I'd like to thank my friend Ed Gilbert who was a source of inexhaustible inspiration and knowledge on the subject. He himself, his wife Cathy, and their children, gave me a quantity of documents of which a good number were used to enrich these pages.

Ken Estes also shared his archives and supplied a large number of documents. A true "Bible" on the subject of the mechanized history of the U.S. Marine Corps, Ken patiently answered all my questions over the years.

The veterans and their families, as well as sharing their memories, shared photos taken covertly on the battlefield. Their names are listed in the "Interviews" section of this book.

The personnel of the American institutions have also given precious help locating the photographs and films needed for this publication: the American National Archive (NARA), the Marine Corps History Division (USMC HD), the National Museum of the Pacific War (NMPW), the University of South Carolina (USC), and the Naval History & Heritage Command.

A number of other people took part in the realization of this book by sharing information, photos, or contacts with veterans or institutions. This is the case for (by alphabetical order of first names):

Alisa Whitley, Andrew Figallo, Annette Amerman, Becky Quine-Auvil, Chuck Bernard, Dan Formella, Dave Vickers, David Doyle, Dona Pearson-Werner, Fred Allison, George Proulx, Greg Wilsbacher, James Mason, Kim Harrison, Kirby Nave, Mike and Jack Livingston, Mike Hogan, Morgan Gillard, Peter Flahavin, PJ and Mark Navarro, Robert Moore, Scott Freund, Sean Winn, Sharon Van Riper, Steve McCloud, Steve Zaloga.

With talent, Candice Pangaud reproduced the mascot of C Company of the 2nd Tank Battalion for the specific needs of the project. Eric Schwartz realized with brio the color profiles which have enriched this book.

Finally, I would like to thank my wife, my son, and my mother for their patience in the face of this overcrowding pastime. Caroline, my wife, conscientiously helped me to digitalize hundreds of documents in the American archives. I thank her warmly for that.